The Devil
And How to Resist Him

Also available from
Sophia Institute Press
by Gerald Vann:

The Seven Sweet Blessings of Christ
(And How to Make Them Yours)

The Devil
And How to Resist Him

by
Gerald Vann, O.P.
and
P. K. Meagher, O.P.

SOPHIA INSTITUTE PRESS®
Manchester, New Hampshire

The Devil: And How to Resist Him was originally published in English in 1957 in London by HarperCollins Ltd. under the title Stones or Bread? and in New York by Sheed and Ward under the title The Temptations of Christ. This 1997 edition is published with the permission of HarperCollins. The Author asserts the moral right to be identified as the Author of this work.

The cover painting is a detail from The Temptations of Christ by Titian (Titiano Vecellio). Photo courtesy of Scala/Art Resource, New York.

Sophia Institute Press®
Box 5284, Manchester, NH 03108
1-800-888-9344

Nihil Obstat: Fr. Kieran Mulvey, O.P., S.T.L., M.A.,
Fr. Drostan MacLaren, O.P., S.T.L., M.A.
Imprimi Potest: Fr. Hilary Carpenter, O.P., Prior Provincialis
June 12, 1957
Nihil Obstat: John M. T. Barton, S.T.D., L.S.S., Censor Deputatus
Imprimatur: George L. Craven, Vicarius Generalis, Sebastopolis
Westmonasterii, July 19, 1957

Library of Congress Cataloging-in-Publication Data

Vann, Gerald, 1906-1963.
  [Stones or bread?]
  The Devil : and how to resist him / by Gerald Vann and P. K. Meagher.
    p.   cm.
  Originally published: Stones or bread? London : HarperCollins, 1957.
  Includes bibliographical references.
  ISBN 0-918477-61-1 (pbk. : alk. paper)
  1. Jesus Christ — Temptation. 2. Temptation. I. Meagher, P. K.
    (Paul Kevin) II. Title.
  BT355.V3   1997
  232.9'5 — dc21   97-35411 CIP

97 98 99 00 01 02 10 9 8 7 6 5 4 3 2 1

Contents

Editor's Note: The biblical references in the following pages are based on the Douay-Rheims and Ronald Knox versions of the Old and New Testaments. Where applicable, quotations have been cross-referenced with the differing names and enumeration in the Revised Standard Version, using the following symbol: (RSV =).

The Devil
And How to Resist Him

Introduction

Do you believe in the Devil?

It seems probable that a large number of modern Christians would be somewhat embarrassed if faced with the question. Many would like to see in Satan only a symbolic representation of the evil tendencies in human nature. Others, while giving a notional assent to his existence, could hardly be said to believe effectively in him, to make that belief an active element in their lives: their assent would remain notional rather than real.

Certainly it seems that the Devil is rather played down in modern Christian teaching and writing, and we tend to discount stories, such as we find in the lives of the saints, in which he makes a personal appearance.

It seems useful to inquire why this is so.

Our purpose in this book is to study the temptations of our Lord, and the lessons to be learned from them would be there whether we took the account of them in the Gospels as historical fact or pure symbol. But to take the story simply as symbol is to rob it of a great deal of its depth. And granted that Satan does exist, it would be extremely foolish and dangerous to write him off as mere fantasy. Indeed, as the writer Denis de Rougemont has pointed out, Satan's great triumph in modern times consists precisely in having caused mankind to disbelieve in him. For if Satan is as mighty and malicious, as close to us, and as intent on our destruction as Christian tradition would have us believe, nothing could be more foolhardy than to pretend he does not exist at all.

Moreover it is a short step from disbelief in Satan to disbelief in the reality of moral evil in any form, to the view that there is never anything morally censurable in crime: that it is simply a disease, as wanting in moral significance as measles or a cold, and to be cured simply by proper medical or psychiatric treatment. Sin, too, as distinguished from the more obvious and violent forms of antisocial behavior which we call crime, has lost most of its meaning and become largely a question of outmoded social conventions or obscurantist prejudices.

Such a climate of opinion may well influence Christians, who live in it, more deeply and in more ways than they realize. It is possible, while acknowledging the reality of sin, to adopt in practice a somewhat cavalier attitude toward it, as something regrettable, of course, but inevitable and not worth all the fuss the theologians and devout writers make about it.

And where Satan is concerned, it is all too easy to accept his existence in a vague and wholly theoretical sort of way while in practice ignoring it. We are often "tempted," yes; but for the source of the temptation we need look no farther than ourselves. We know so much more nowadays than was known, for instance, in the Middle Ages about our own urges and impulses and motivations. Medieval man, aware of the up-surge of some sinful impulse in him, looked around for a demon, with horns and tail, to explain it; Freud[1] and others have changed all that for us.

But there is something very naive and unreal about any such clear-cut distinction between temptations which spring simply from our own inclination to evil and others which might be supposed to be due entirely to the promptings of Satan. In the first place, if Satan does exist and is what Christianity holds him to be, he is far too intelligent to tempt us to forms of evil to which we have no inclination: on the contrary, he will seek to utilize our own particular propensities.

Secondly, we have to accept those propensities as realities within ourselves, yes; but how did they get there? If we look just at the imperfections, the quirks of character, in our friends and in ordinary, decent people, we may well fail to discern any sign of diabolical activity. But what if we take a larger view? If we look at the appalling burden of physical and mental anguish which weighs down the world, and at the still more appalling cruelty, malice, and stark evil which cause so much of it, shall we be so ready to believe that all this is sufficiently explained from within humanity — the humanity we know as normally so decent, so good?

We can invoke, plausibly and indeed validly enough, the psychology of sadism to explain one case of murderousness; this criminal is a diseased man just as surely as the victim of cancer or tuberculosis, and the one simply needs psychiatric treatment

---

[1]   Sigmund Freud (1856-1939), Austrian physicist and neurologist who founded psychoanalysis.

The Devil

as the other needs medical treatment. But then multiply the one example, as we have to, by millions. There is not just something wrong with one man or with a few men; our whole world is a diseased, twisted world, and against the goodness of so many ordinary, decent folk you must set the vastness and the inhuman horror of the evils they are powerless to prevent or to stop: the Buchenwalds[2] and torture-chambers, the slave labor camps, the massacres and mass deportations, and the modern techniques — tortures, drugs, and inverted psychiatry — that destroy not merely men's bodies but their minds. And then it becomes less easy to write Satan off as a medieval superstition.

Why, then, do we find it so hard to take the Devil seriously? The question was studied in an interesting essay by Professor Henri Irénée Marrou entitled "*Un ange déchu, un ange pourtant*" ("A fallen angel, yet still an angel.")[3] He suggests that the difficulty springs from the fact that we are not really thinking of Satan at all, but of a phantasma, a caricature, against which it is natural enough, and indeed laudable, to react, for it represents not the Devil of Christian theology, but the principle of evil of Gnosticism: as God is wholly good, is indeed *the* Good, so we think of Satan as wholly evil, as Evil the adversary on more or less equal terms with the Good. Add to this the effect on us of medieval paintings and legends of devils with horns and tails, of Mephistopheles,[4] and of the creations of a

---

[2] Buchenwald was the site of a Nazi concentration camp and extermination center in southwest East Germany.

[3] *Satan*, Études Carmélitaines (Paris: Desclée de Brouwer, 1948), 28 ff.

[4] The devil in the legend of Faust.

Hieronymus Bosch,[5] and it is easy to see how the resultant figure seems wildly improbable to us.

We have to remember, first of all, that according to Christian thought, evil is nonbeing — a privation. Satan therefore is not evil, pure and simple, as God is pure goodness: he is an angel, and his fall did not destroy his angelic nature. So it is that some early Christian paintings depict him as a beautiful winged youth; after all, his biblical name, Lucifer, the "light-bearer," underlines this idea of beauty, of dazzling splendor.

He is said in many stories to have appeared to men under monstrous shapes; but these are momentary disguises designed to inspire terror, and are no more a representation of Satan's angelic nature than the simpering, epicene, winged young men of modern repository art are a faithful representation of the good angels.

In the second place, we have to remember that if we find it hard to believe in the fallen angels, we will find it hard to believe in angels at all. That is part of the penalty we pay for our pervasive materialism. Like doubting Thomas, we are reluctant to believe in anything we cannot see or touch.[6] As Marrou points out, except perhaps for the idea of guardian angels, Christian angelology means very little to us; and he points in particular to the eclipse in modern times of the archangel Michael compared with his important cultus in the Middle Ages.

We might well remind ourselves, therefore, that in this, as in so much else, we are almost alone in the world's history in

[5] Jerome van Aken (c. 1450-1516), Dutch painter.
[6] John 20:25.

the impoverishment to which our materialism has led us; we might remind ourselves that it is, to say the least, somewhat arrogant to suppose that in the unimaginable vastness of the universe, we humans are the sole intelligent creatures, perched improbably as we are on the tiny speck of dust we call the earth. We should be far better equipped for life, and should find life far more interesting, if we were more aware of Jacob's ladder[7] and had the sense to understand the Christian reality faintly adumbrated in the naiads and dryads of the Greeks.

We would be better equipped to deal with evil and its effects if we realized that while the kingdom of God is within us, the kingdom of Satan can be within us too; and that the Greek satyrs, whom we meet also in the book of Isaiah,[8] should suggest to us something much deeper and more sinister than a mere pagan lewdness. They should suggest something somber and subhumanly degraded, but satanic too; for the satyr is the symbol of man half-dehumanized, half turned into a goat. But traditionally it is the goat who is adored in the witches' sabbats, for it is the purpose of the warped but still mighty superhuman spirit to rob us of our humanity so as to make it impossible for us to know divinity.

We are indebted to C. S. Lewis[9] for an imaginative presentation of the angelic nature far nearer to reality than the conceptions of the repository artists, and we would do well to reconstruct our mental image of Satan accordingly: an angel like the others, but malignant, his mighty nature wholly given

[7] Gen. 28:12.

[8] Isa. 13:21.

[9] British Christian writer and author of *The Screwtape Letters* (1898-1963).

over to the pursuit of evil. God created free beings, beings therefore endowed with the terrible power of retreating from reality into nothingness if they so willed — for, once again, evil is privation, nonbeing, emptiness — and Satan is simply the first of those beings to choose this path. We moderns, with our somber understanding of the will-to-death, should not find that conception so remote from our ordinary ways of thought. We have our own *nostalgie de la boue:*[10] it is simply the urge to do in our own more brutish way what Satan, in all the majesty of his giant intellect, did in his.

The extreme expression of that nostalgia is to be found in that worship of Satan which is part of human history and is far from being extinct at the present day. We may write off a great deal of demonology and witchcraft as mere moonshine. The fact remains that underneath all that, there is a hard core of hatred of God and servitude to His greatest enemy; there is all the horror and blasphemy of the Black Mass, and the fact of the ravaged souls and psychotic frenzies of its hierophants.

Where all else fails, terror may be the last remaining motive of credibility. There is certainly nothing unreasonable or infantile about a fear inspired by the Mystery of Iniquity; but whatever else it may be, that Mystery cannot be ultimate Reality: to believe in Satan is to be logically committed to belief in God.[11]

But to believe in the Devil is not to believe that every time we are conscious of an evil impulse in ourselves, we must see in

[10] "Nostalgia for the mud": a longing for depravity.
[11] Cf. Gerald Vann, *The High Green Hill* (New York: Sheed and Ward, 1951), ch. 11.

it the direct influence of Satan himself. Christian angelology tells us simply that the visible world we apprehend through our senses is not the only reality with which we are in contact; that in that visible world there is another world of mighty spirits, some filled with love of God and striving to help the world through its travail to its ultimate fulfillment in God, and others filled with hatred of God and striving to destroy the world with that hatred and its effects.

It is that evil power that covers the world, as St. Augustine[12] puts it, as though with an *aer caliginosus*, a pall of dense, murky vapor, shutting out the light of the sun. We speak of being black-hearted: that is what happens when the vapor finds entry into the soul, and we know well enough the horrors, the degradation, and the disintegration to which it can lead. We do well, then, to recognize Satan for what he really is.

In the case of our own temptations, we should certainly be ill-advised to try to distinguish between those which are of immediate satanic origin and those which are not. The important thing is that they are all of satanic origin in the sense that ultimately they all spring from the evil which has twisted and warped the soul of humanity, from that Mystery of Iniquity which is not to be explained in terms of humanity itself. When, then, we think of the story of our Lord's temptations, we can for practical purposes, when applying it to our own experience, think of Satan simply in terms of those evil suggestions and impulses, rising up within us, with which we are so familiar.

[12] Bishop of Hippo and Doctor of the Church (354-430).

Introduction

But we are wise to remind ourselves of the mighty power of evil from which they ultimately spring; we are wise to remember the words in which St. Paul warns us: "It is not against flesh and blood that we enter the lists; we have to do with princedoms and powers, with those who have mastery of the world in these dark days, with malign influences in an order higher than ours."[13] For only if we are persuaded of that shall we be moved to obey St. Paul's bidding and take up the armor of God so that we may be able to stand our ground when the evil time comes.[14]

We do well to fear the might and malice of Satan, and this story can teach us, among many other things, the fear that we need.

[13] Eph. 6:12 (Ronald Knox translation).
[14] Eph. 6:13.

Chapter One

Was Christ Really Tempted?

It is strange that the Gospel story of the tempting of Christ in the desert[15] seems to have been so little used by spiritual writers as material for meditation, for in many ways, it is ideal for the purpose. It is full of significant detail, demanding an almost word-by-word study. Moreover, in its symbolism we can see represented the whole life and ministry of Jesus. Father Lagrange[16] sees it as resembling a prologue to a play of Euripides, a prologue in two voices, explaining the events which are to follow in the drama and pointing the moral; or again, it is like those overtures which weave a preliminary pattern out of the musical themes which will form the substance of the succeeding opera.

Thus, for all its brevity, the story is comprehensive, and that very fact makes it ideal for meditation, for it safeguards us against a danger inherent in any prolonged concentration on

---

[15] Matt. 4:1-11; Mark 1:12-13; Luke 4:1-13.

[16] Marie-Joseph Lagrange (1855-1938), Dominican Bible scholar.

one particular theme in the Gospel narrative: the danger of isolating the theme and seeing it out of proportion because we have taken it out of its proper setting in the story as a whole. And the brevity of the narrative in its turn can also be of great help to us: in any attempt at concentration (as we know all too well), the human mind is liable to fly off at a tangent at the first presentation of some extraneous interest; but here there are no extraneous details to distract us, so that we can let ourselves follow freely the various trains of thought the narrative may suggest and yet be kept by them to a basic unity of attention and purpose.

Finally, the theme of temptation is obviously one in which we are deeply concerned: "The life of man upon earth is a warfare,"[17] and temptation is the actual clash of arms in which its issues are decided. And Christ's temptations cannot but be of vital interest to us because, in a sense, His temptation and His victory were also ours. "He transformed us into Himself when He willed to be tempted by Satan," St. Augustine tells us. "For in Christ you were tempted. He took flesh from you for Himself, and from Him to you there came salvation. From you He took death upon Himself, and from Him to you there came victory. . . . He could have kept the tempter from Him; but had He not been tempted, He would not have given you who face temptation the power to overcome."[18]

The three accounts given to us by the synoptists are very similar. Mark, as is to be expected, is very concise, but in his two short verses he manages to include all the essentials of the

---

[17] Job 7:1.
[18] On Ps. 60, Patrologia Latina 36, col. 724.

story: the Spirit, Christ, the desert, the beasts, the forty days, Satan, the tempting, and the ministering angels. Matthew and Luke, with their greater detail, differ from each other in only one important respect: the inversion in Luke of the order of the second and third temptations as recorded in Matthew. There is no wholly satisfactory explanation of this difference. Most authorities hold that Matthew is following a chronological order of events, and Luke a logical sequence of ideas. Some suggest that it was St. Luke's intention to make the scenes of the successive temptations correspond to the successive scenes of Christ's ministry.[19]

However this may be, there is a problem of greater importance at which we ought to glance, and that is the question of the precise *nature* of the events which make up the story. That the story itself is, in fact, history we take for granted: for us, the Gospels are historical books, and what they narrate as facts we take as such. But when it comes to assessing the precise nature of the historical events here recorded, opinion is divided.

The ancient writers generally held that temptation came to our Lord through His outer senses: what happened, happened visibly and audibly: Satan appeared to Him visibly in human form — had he not appeared visibly to Adam in the form of a serpent? — spoke to Him in an audible voice, and physically transported Him to the pinnacle of the temple and the summit of the high mountain.

True, these latter details were not accepted literally by all: some thought it unfitting and therefore unbelievable that

---

[19] Joseph-Mary Vosté, *De Tentatione Christi*, *Studia Theologiae Biblicae* (Rome: Angelicum, 1934), 67-69.

The Devil

Christ should be literally carried or led by Satan. "It is unbelievable," wrote Origen,[20] "that the Devil should lead the Son of God or that He should follow. If He *followed,* surely it was as an athlete, who sets out of his own volition to his trial of strength." Again, the "high mountain" presents yet greater difficulty, for in Palestine no such mountain exists.

Moreover, in St. Luke's version, the Devil is said to have shown Jesus all the kingdoms of the world in a moment of time, a phrase more readily understood of an imaginative than of a physical vision. And as time went by, the view that the temptations were at least in part a matter of internal suggestion rather than of outward occurrences found increasing favor, and today is commonly held among exegetes.

For, indeed, the idea that Satan appeared to our Lord in human form is not derived directly from the text of the Gospels; and no such apparition is mentioned anywhere else in the Scriptures to lead us to suppose that the same thing would have happened here. We are told, of course, that Satan came and spoke to Jesus and took Him to the Temple and the high mountain, and in Matthew and Luke we are given the actual words of the dialogue; but nothing is more common than the description of the events of inner consciousness in terms of outward, material reality. We say that a thought *comes* to mind and, when we understand something, that we *see;* conscience is a *voice* within us, and we are *carried away* by our thoughts and feelings. Often such metaphors can be avoided only by the use of ponderous circumlocutions. And if we find

[20] Alexandrian biblical critic, exegete, theologian, and spiritual writer (c. 185-254).

nothing strange in "angelic speech," on which the theologians love to dwell, or in the picture of the seraphim crying out to one another in holy song,[21] it certainly should not seem to us far-fetched to find Satan's communication with a human consciousness described in terms of speech even though no words were actually spoken.

So too with his coming and departing, which aptly enough describe his initiation and final abandonment of a struggle with a soul. Our Lord Himself was later to say, "The Prince of this world cometh"[22] when the reference is clearly to an outburst of Satan's invisible activity rather than to a visible, corporeal appearance; indeed, the two comings are linked by the words with which St. Luke concludes his account of the temptation: "And all the temptation being ended, the Devil departed from Him for a time";[23] the later coming being a continuation of the conflict begun in the desert.

Moreover, to take the story as referring to events in the external world is to commit ourselves to a number of details which would require preternatural explanation, and this we should hesitate to do where the text does not compel us. There is no such necessity here; for a physical interpretation of the details of temple pinnacle and mountain summit gives nothing to the story which is not as well or better supplied by the interpretation in terms of inner consciousness.

It is true that some theologians are reluctant to accept any reading of the temptations which would make them an assault

[21] Isa. 6:3.
[22] John 14:30.
[23] Luke 4:13.

The Devil

on the internal senses of our Lord. We certainly cannot think that Satan was capable of influencing His rational powers; but the same is true, according to these theologians, of His imagination, the highest of the sense-faculties and one so closely associated with reason that in Jesus it must have been equally immune from attack. Yet it cannot be denied that such an attack was possible if our Lord permitted it, as He permitted Himself to be attacked through His outward senses; and if it is thought "unfitting" that the Son of God should thus be assailed by Satan, it was surely much more "unfitting" that He should be scourged and buffeted and crucified: yet "ought not Christ to have suffered these things?"[24]

It is, moreover, very difficult to see how the temptations could have influenced our Lord's outward senses only: you cannot thus departmentalize the elements in consciousness; you cannot ignore the inseparability of outward and inner sensibility or the normal interplay of external and internal sense-functions.

Some authorities, then, are of the opinion that the temptations were a purely inward experience. Thus Emile Le Camus writes that Satan "must have spoken the language of spirits, in our opinion, and through suggestions, terrible influences, he must have solicited His soul interiorly; it was in the imagination that he placed Him on the pinnacle of the temple and on the mountain, and it was before His mind only that he made the kingdoms of the world and the depths of the abyss to be in evidence. No more was needed to try Jesus. Physical reality would add nothing to the temptation. The Savior could not

[24] Luke 24:26.

have conquered with greater glory, nor could Satan have failed with more disgrace."[25] It might be added that this purely internal mode of temptation would seem to be far more probable in itself, corresponding as it does with our own normal human experience (we do not normally expect our struggles with evil to involve a combat with a visible and tangible adversary) and, being thus closer to us, it is more likely to bring home to us the lessons which our Lord's experience holds for us.

However, the problem remains unsolved and insoluble, and opinion continues to be divided. As Father Lagrange, who himself inclined to the view that the temptations were in part external and visible,[26] pointed out: "One might say that the whole episode of the temptation is enveloped in a sort of cloud, so that the precise details are not clearly visible";[27] and perhaps we are meant to take that obscurity itself as a lesson, a warning against being distracted by unessential elements in the story. For in whatever manner Satan's suggestions were made, the significance of the combat remains the same; and it is with this that we who ponder the story are concerned.

St. Paul tells us: "For in that, wherein He Himself hath suffered and been tempted, He is able to succor them also that

[25] Emile Paul Constant Le Camus, *The Life of Christ*, trans. Rt. Rev. William A. Hickey (New York: The Cathedral Library Assoc., 1923), Vol. 1, 267.

[26] Marie-Joseph Lagrange, *Evangile Selon Saint Luc* (Paris: J. Gabalda), ed. 3, 134-136.

[27] Lagrange, *The Gospel of Jesus Christ* (London: Burns, Oates, and Washbourne, 1938), vol. 1, 83.

are tempted"; and again, "We have not a high priest who cannot have compassion on our infirmities: but one tempted like as we are, without sin."[28] The Scriptures themselves thus assure us that Christ's temptation is meant to be a comfort to us, a source of strength and victory. We, in our struggles, are to look with confidence for help; for as St. Gregory the Great expresses it, His temptation was meant to overcome our temptations, just as His death overcomes our own.[29]

Our Lord, then, was really tempted; His struggle was a real struggle. Yet how are we to reconcile this fact with all that we know of the perfection of His human nature? We know Him as "full of grace and truth";[30] we know Him as perfect in knowledge, incapable of sin, free of all taint of evil desires: how, then, can He be tempted as we are?

This question has led some writers to attempt to safeguard the perfection of Christ by minimizing the reality of the temptation; and in so doing, they rob it of a great part of its power to help, encourage, and inspire us. But their fears are surely unfounded. The death of our Lord was a stark and terrible one: beaten, bruised, and tortured, He died, on a Cross. The brutal facts cannot be ignored or minimized; yet we do not imagine that His human perfection or His divinity lessened the horror of the Passion: on the contrary, we believe that they added to its intensity. We are not worried there by any incompatibility between perfection and degradation: why, then, should we be worried in the case of the temptation? We

[28] Heb. 2:18, 4:15.
[29] St. Gregory I (Pope and Doctor of the Church; c. 540-604), Homily 16 on the Gospels.
[30] John 1:14.

are told that our Lord was tempted, and that must mean that He lived through the inward struggle, the agony, which temptation can mean for us all.

Christ was "tempted in all things like as we are, without sin." Now, it is true that we tend to think of our experience of sin as playing a large part in our experience of temptation; and indeed the leaning toward evil which is the legacy of past wrongdoing can add greatly to the force of a present temptation. But the connection is not a necessary or universal one. Essentially the force of a temptation depends on the force of one's inward feelings, and these can be very powerful quite apart from any previous experience of sin. And when they are, the man who resists to the end is likely to know far more about their force than the man who yields; for the latter gives in before he has felt what he knows to be the final strain: it is the former who sees the upheaval through to the end, to its final intensity.

But when we speak of the sinlessness of Christ, we mean more than that His life was free from all sinful acts: we are excluding also all those disorderly impulses which we call concupiscence. The lusting of flesh against spirit is not altogether free from sin. Hence St. Thomas Aquinas points out how appropriate it was that Christ's temptation should come to Him by suggestion from without, since it shows us clearly that it involved no evil impulse within His own nature.[31]

The fact remains that when we, for our part, find ourselves incited to evil from without, the incitement does not remain

---

[31] St. Thomas Aquinas (Dominican philosopher, theologian, and Doctor of the Church; c. 1225-1274), *Summa Theologica*, III, Q. 41, art. 1.

entirely external to us, or, if it does, we do not think of it as a real temptation. When we do not feel drawn, attracted, we are not truly tempted; when, on the other hand, we do feel an inner attraction corresponding to the outward suggestion, it is either because our wills are already disposed to evil or because the suggestion awakens and stirs our concupiscence. In the case of our Lord, any such cooperation is unthinkable: His will was unalterably fixed upon good, and He was wholly free from concupiscence.

If, then, for Him, the external suggestion evoked no such inward response, how can we say that He was truly tempted as we are? And what would be the point of the dramatic preparation for the struggle, the forty days' fast? And how can St. Paul encourage us to take heart, when beset by our own very real temptations, because we have a High Priest who, having been tempted in all things like as we are, has learned to have compassion on our infirmities?

The answer is a simple one, and it is to be found in the psychology of temptation. The narrative tells us nothing of our Lord's inner reactions to Satan's suggestions; we are merely told how He rebutted them. But we have only to turn for a moment to the account of His final great temptation in the garden of Gethsemane to see how deep and searing His inner agony could be. Here in the desert as there in the garden, He could feel to the full the pain and dismay which normally follow the frustration of our desire for what is congenial to us or the necessity of choosing what is repugnant.

Now, it might be argued that what filled Him with horror in His agony in Gethsemane was the prospect of suffering and death, from which human nature legitimately recoils, whereas here in the desert, the suggestions made to Him were evil and there could be no question of a legitimate inclination toward them. But this objection implies something about temptation which is simply not true. It implies that temptation is an invitation to evil and nothing else, so that any appetitive response evoked by it must be sinful. But the temptations of which we ourselves have experience seldom consist in a bare proposal of something evil; they are more subtle than that; the evil suggestion is woven into a complex texture of thoughts and desires which are quite lawful.

Our attention may be fixed on some object which in itself is both innocent and desirable, or on something hard and painful from which it is legitimate to recoil: in either case the emotions will naturally be aroused and perhaps powerfully engaged, and this is a normal and important element in temptation. So far, no evil has been done; the feelings involved are natural and unexceptionable, but the ground has been prepared for the evil suggestion to take root. Can the desire be fulfilled, or the feeling of repulsion be acted upon? The mind intervenes to pass judgment; and the judgment, because of some moral obstacle, is unfavorable: the emotions cannot be satisfied without defying God's will. So the soul becomes a battleground: the senses or emotions pulling in one direction, the mind and will in another; and because of the emotional involvement, the voice of reason or the appeal to the will of God will seem to be a shackling of freedom.

Now, the man who loves God deeply may accept the frustration of his desires with perfect resignation, but that is not to say that the acceptance will be easy or painless. On the contrary, it may amount to real agony of soul; the more so inasmuch as the previous concentration of attention on the thing desired but now to be rejected will have aroused the feelings to a high pitch of intensity. But the pain and bitterness involve no defiance of God's will, no moral imperfection, any more than would the grief, the desolation, experienced by some holy person at the loss of a dearly loved friend.

Now, with us, the shackling of natural desires often enough produces rebellion; the thwarted feelings rise up to color the judgment and seduce the will. In Christ this certainly could not take place: His senses and feelings could exert no subversive influence on His mind and will. So it is, as we have seen, that the suggestion of evil had of necessity to come to Him from without. And the suggestion once made could not stir up disorderly impulses within Him to add to its force. He could not, as we can and so often do, cooperate with Satan.

But if we see our Lord's temptation, not simply as a suggestion of something evil, but as a directing of His attention to the difficulties, the hardships and pain and agony, which His life and ministry were to involve, and on the other hand, to the ease with which He could win success and glory by a change of plan, then we can see readily enough how this could indeed have been an agonizing experience for Him, a temptation really comparable to our own and one great enough to account for the significance attached to it by St. Paul. Here, as in the garden, His human flesh could legitimately — and indeed must necessarily — shrink from the evil things, the pain and anguish, which faced Him; and the good things to which His attention was drawn were in themselves very appealing: why indeed should He not bring His people overwhelmingly to accept Him, and therefore His message, by a simple exercise of His power and thus spare Himself all the toil of the ministry and all the torture of the Passion? That His emotions should be so engaged, when God's will and His own deliberate human choice were opposed to their satisfaction, is no more proof of any concupiscence in Him than is His agony of soul in the garden, when fear and horror swept over Him at the thought of what lay ahead, even though His deliberate choice was fixed on the very thing He dreaded. Psychologically speaking, the two experiences were in substance the same.

But if all this is so, are we not obliged at least to admit that our Lord's sense-desires and feelings, drawn as they were in a direction opposite to that of reason and will, were therefore in some way outside the control of reason? And is not that in itself a sort of concupiscence? No, we must not judge by our own emotional disorders. When we, for our part, experience this conflict of impulses, we have to admit that our lower impulses are outside the control of the higher, at least in the sense that they exist not because we want them to be as they are, but in spite of our wishes.

In our Lord, on the other hand, the conflict was entirely voluntary; He *wanted to feel it*. He deliberately allowed His flesh to recoil from the pain of the Passion in order to taste to the full the bitterness of His chalice. Similarly we are to suppose that He willed to experience to the full all the suffering involved in the ordeal of temptation so as to be as close as possible to all His fellowmen. "Wherefore it behooved Him in all things to be made like unto His brethren, that He might become a merciful and faithful High Priest before God, that He might be a propitiation for the sins of the people. For in that, wherein He Himself hath suffered and been tempted, He is able to succor them also that are tempted."[32]

Our Lord's senses and feelings, then, were not outside the control of His reason and will when He was tempted; but there certainly was a contradiction, a real struggle, and it is in this that the essential tension of temptation lies. This is made clear by St. Thomas when he asks whether the human will of Christ was in complete conformity with the will of God and answers no. He distinguishes, first of all, between our Lord's sense-appetites, on the one hand, and His will on the other; and then he goes on to make a further distinction between the will in its natural instinctive workings and the will as a reasoned, deliberate choosing. "The Son of God," he tells us, "before His Passion, allowed His flesh to do and suffer all the things proper to it, and similarly with all the powers of His soul. Now, it is clear that the sense-appetites naturally shrink from bodily pain and hurt, and that the will in its natural instinctive workings recoils from what is contrary to nature and in itself an evil, such as death; nevertheless the deliberate will may sometimes choose such things because of some ulterior end." Hence, he concludes, as far as His sense-appetites and natural instinctive will were concerned, Christ "could will something other than the will of God"; and he quotes the words of our Lord Himself in His agony: "Not what I will, but what Thou wilt."[33]

We need not fear, then, to see in Christ's temptations a struggle just as real as our own and infinitely more intense and

---

[32] Heb. 2:17-18.
[33] *Summa Theologica*, III, Q. 18, art. 5; Matt. 26:39.

agonizing; and so, as we can claim fellowship with Him in the struggle, we can also look to Him with confidence for compassion for our weakness, and for the divine strengthening we so often need.

∞

Biblical scholars and ecclesiastical writers have offered various interpretations of our Lord's temptations; and it may help us to glance here at some of the more-notable differences before going on to detailed considerations.

Many of the Fathers of the Church see a significant parallel between the temptation of Christ and that of Adam and Eve. St. Irenaeus drew attention to it in illustration of the "summing up of all things" in Christ.[34]

St. Gregory the Great developed the idea. The ancient enemy, he tells us, assaulted the first man, our proto-parent, in three temptations — to illicit sense-pleasure, to vainglory, and to avarice — and by tempting, the enemy overcame him, subjecting the man to himself. He tempted him to sense-pleasure when he showed him the fruit of the forbidden tree and encouraged him to eat; to vainglory when he told him, "Ye shall be as gods";[35] and to avarice when he spoke of knowing good and evil, for it is avarice which sets our aim too high. He failed, however, in his approach to the New Man, although his strategy was the same as that which had succeeded with the old. He tempted to sense-pleasure when he said, "Command

---

[34] St. Irenaeus (bishop of Lyons; c. 130-200), *Contra Haereses*, v. 21, *Patrologia Graeca* 7, col. 1179-1182.

[35] Gen. 3:5.

that these stones be made bread"; to vainglory when he said, "If Thou art the Son of God, throw Thyself down"; and to ambition when, pointing out all the kingdoms of the world, he said, "All these will I give Thee if Thou wilt fall down and worship me."[36]

The same interpretation is to be found in St. Ambrose[37] and St. Augustine among the Latin Fathers and in St. John Chrysostom[38] among the Greeks, and thenceforth it is used by practically all the commentators until the close of the Middle Ages and is still favored by many authors today. Other modern authorities, however, see the temptations and the logical connection between them quite differently. Godet, for instance, who favors the order found in St. Luke, sees the first temptation as referring to the humanity of Jesus, the second as referring to His messianic work, and the third to His divine power.[39] Others who prefer the same order think of our Lord as tempted to an inordinate use of power in ascending grades: over inanimate nature, over men, and over God Himself.[40] Others again see the temptations as assailing Jesus in body, mind, and spirit,[41] or as invoking the concupiscence of the flesh, the concupiscence of the eyes, and the pride of life.

[36] *Homilies on the Gospels*, Bk. 1, Homily 16 on Matthew 4:1-11, *Patrologia Latina* 76, col. 1135-1138.

[37] Bishop of Milan and Doctor of the Church (c. 339-397).

[38] Bishop of Constantinople and Doctor of the Church (c. 347-407).

[39] Frédéric Louis Godet, *Commentaire sur l'Evangile de Saint Luc*, 2nd ed. (Paris: Sandoz and Fischbacher, 1872), vol. 1, 266, 271, 274.

[40] Br. Violet, *Der Aufbau der Versuchungsgeschichte Jesu* (Harnack-Ehrung, 1921), 19.

[41] Hastings, "Notes on Recent Exposition," *Expository Times* 14 (1902-3): 389.

Was Christ Really Tempted?

But by far the greatest number of present-day commentators are agreed in seeing in the temptations something much more than solicitations such as might be used to corrupt an ordinary man. Jesus was the Messiah and, at the time when the temptations occurred, was on the point of beginning His messianic ministry. Most modern exegetes, then, are of the opinion that Satan's purpose was to seduce our Lord from fulfilling that ministry in the manner willed by His Father.

The Jewish people had, in the course of time, so distorted the teachings of the prophets that, by our Lord's day, the Messiah of popular expectation was a purely worldly figure: a great king, a national hero and liberator who would free them from the yoke of the Gentiles and give them dominion over the peoples of the earth. Satan's suggestion, then, was that Jesus should yield to this popular messianism and become what the people looked for: let Him win the people to Himself (and, of course, to God) in a way which would really be successful. It would, moreover, mean a glorious career; it would be simple to accomplish and congenial to His human nature; it would avoid all the trials and contradictions foretold by Isaiah. After all, surely it *was* God's will that He should be the King of the Jews: what more reasonable than that He should adopt the means most likely to bring this about in actual fact?

So, as we shall see, Satan urges our Lord to accept first a part and then the whole of this worldly program, which, of course, offered no threat to his own objectives in the world of men. But Jesus rebuffs the tempter: He will carry out His ministry as His Father wills it to be done; He will not be exempted from the sufferings and trials of other men; He will not resort to stupendous exhibitions of power in order to force

The Devil

an allegiance from His fellowmen; He will have nothing of the glorious kingship of popular imagination, for His kingdom is not of this world.

Thus at the very beginning of Christ's ministry, the temptations foreshadow and summarize that long conflict which was to go on throughout the next three years: the conflict between the true and the false messianism, and between the blindness of the people and His own obedience to His Father.

Chapter Two

The Contenders

"What went you out into the desert to see?" our Lord asked the multitudes who had flocked from Jerusalem and all Judea and the country about the Jordan to hear the preaching of John the Baptist.[42]

We may ask ourselves the same question as we set out to follow Jesus into the desert and to watch as He prays and fasts and finally enters into combat with Satan: what exactly are we going to see?

The object of our Lord's work in the world was to restore God's creation to its original perfection. We live in a fallen, twisted world because of the cunning of the Serpent; and so it was decreed that the first step in the work of re-creation should be the humbling of the Serpent, his head bruised by the Seed of the Woman,[43] so that the work of restoring humanity might follow, step by step, the order of its fall.

---

[42] Matt. 11:7, 3:5.

[43] The better interpretation of the Hebrew of Gen. 3:15.

The Devil

"For this purpose the Son of God appeared," St. John tells us, "that He might destroy the works of the Devil."[44] And the first of his works to be destroyed was the prestige he had established for himself by his victory in the garden of Eden. If this were not overcome, men might not find the hope and courage necessary to oppose him. So it was that Jesus was led by the Spirit into the desert to meet His adversary and to show dramatically that the power of Hell could not prevail against the strength of Christ.[45]

We are to suppose that Satan had observed enough to make it clear to him that this man of Nazareth was the One whose coming the prophets had foretold, and that therefore his own dominion in the world was now in danger. That Jesus was quite literally the Son of God he cannot have known — cannot, at least, have been certain of — for otherwise it would obviously have been futile to attempt to lead Him into sin. He might indeed have lashed out against divinity, and given vent to his hatred in violence against Christ's humanity; but he would hardly have laid himself open to the humiliation which he must inevitably suffer in any conflict with God.

Ignorant, then, or at least doubtful of the real strength of his opponent, he heard in the voice that spoke from Heaven when Jesus was baptized a call to action.[46] He was the Prince of this world; he would not lightly relinquish his dominion. And if his subtlety had seduced so successfully the first human beings for all their rich endowments of nature and grace, why

---

[44] 1 John 3:8.

[45] Cf. Matt. 16:18.

[46] Matt. 3:17; Mark 1:11; Luke 3:22.

should he not also succeed now against this much-heralded champion of humanity?

The story of the temptation is revealed to us because it was so important that we should know of it. There were no witnesses to tell the evangelists what they had seen or heard; they can only have known of it, therefore, either by direct revelation or, more probably, because Jesus Himself had told it to the Apostles. True, "all Scripture, inspired of God, is profitable to teach,"[47] but some parts of it more obviously than others are given for our instruction in matters which concern us closely. The very fact that this purely personal experience of our Lord is given to us underlines its practical importance for us: underlines the fact that it has much to tell us that we need to know about God's love for us, about the struggle which this life involves for us, and about our hope of victory and the means we should adopt to overcome the adversary.

Christ's victory is the guarantee of our own; but that does not mean that we have no more fighting to do. On the contrary, life on earth is a warfare; and we can expect that if Satan dared to challenge Christ, he will be a good deal bolder and more confident where we are concerned. His object in attempting to master Christ was to keep humanity within his power; he failed, but it is still open to him to redeem his failure by continuing to corrupt and destroy individual human beings.

Life on earth is a warfare, and St. Paul bids the Christian think of himself as a soldier of Christ whose business it is to fight a good fight.[48] We have, then, a professional interest in

[47] 2 Tim. 3:16.
[48] 2 Tim. 2:4, 4:7; 1 Tim. 6:12.

what we shall see if we follow Jesus into the wilderness: in observing Satan's weapons and style of attack, and the strategy with which our Lord defended Himself.

But before we go on to consider in detail the events recorded for us, let us glance for a moment at the two combatants and at the role played by the Spirit in the struggle.

In the case of our Lord, we need not dwell on the essential truths regarding His divine and human natures with which we are so familiar; but there is a particular quality in Him which this story reveals and which commands our consideration since it helps us to understand the story more fully.

It is clear that Christ went *voluntarily* to meet His enemy. Indeed, as some commentators have observed, His going into the desert and His forty days' fast almost give the impression that He was challenging a hesitant adversary to come forth and do battle.[49] It is as though He were Himself tempting the tempter. And in this, evidently, His temptation was very unlike ours: for us, temptation is something which comes upon us against our will, whereas for Him it was a contest entered into willingly and even eagerly. This, of course, is true of all the trials which were to confront Christ, as the Scriptures make clear. Pilate would have no power against Him unless it were given him from above.[50] No man was to take His life from Him; only He had the power to lay it down.[51] He went forward eagerly to His Passion: "I have a baptism wherewith I am to be baptized; and how am I straitened until it be

[49] John Maldonatus, *St. Matthew's Gospel,* trans. George J. Davie (London: John Hodges, 1888), ch. 4, part 1.

[50] John 19:11.

[51] John 10:18.

accomplished."[52] And when Peter tried to dissuade Him from choosing a path of sorrow, Jesus rebuked him sternly.[53] So here, too, St. Matthew tells us that His purpose in going into the desert was precisely to be tempted.[54]

Nonetheless, His ordeal was a hard and bitter one. He who as God watches over the sparrows, and who as God-Man had compassion on the multitudes when they were hungry, was Himself tortured with hunger and spent with fatigue from His long watching and praying. Possibly, too, He had to suffer from the heat of the day and the cold by night. St. Mark's inclusion, in his very brief account, of the fact that Jesus was alone with beasts seems to suggest that He knew also the sorrow of loneliness;[55] He was absorbed in prayer, certainly, but there was another occasion when He was similarly absorbed and yet suffered deeply from His loneliness.[56] In His glory, thousands of thousands would minister to Him, and ten thousand times a hundred thousand would stand before Him,[57] but here He is alone with the beasts; and in His loneliness, He seems in a special way to empty Himself and take on the form of a servant.[58]

To this we must add the sense of indignity, perhaps the physical revulsion, caused Him by the approach of the evil spirit. We read that some of the saints were nauseated by the

[52] Luke 12:50.
[53] Mark 8:32-33.
[54] Matt. 4:1.
[55] Mark 1:13.
[56] Matt. 26:40.
[57] Daniel 7:10.
[58] Phil. 2:7.

stench of evil in men: it is not fanciful to suppose an immensely greater revulsion in our Lord at the approach of the source of all the corruption which infects creation. Finally, and above all, there was the agony of soul, caused by the inward struggle, to which we have already alluded: the essence of the temptation itself.

All this pain and distress which our Lord thus deliberately and willingly took upon Himself is the measure both of the gravity of our own situation and of the greatness of His love for us. The test of love is always what the lover does or is prepared to do for the sake of the beloved. That is God's test of our love for Him: "If anyone love me, he will keep my word";[59] "not everyone that saith to me, 'Lord, Lord,' shall enter into the kingdom of Heaven: but he that doth the will of my Father who is in Heaven, he shall enter into the kingdom of Heaven."[60]

It is not enough to protest in fine words that we love; it is not a question of experiencing the warm emotional glow which sometimes passes for love but which in reality is either, at best, the incidental resonance in the body of the strong movement of the will, or, at worst, a purely sensual response which does not flow from the will at all. The test is not what we say or what we feel but what we do. If we look for the perfect love of God, we shall find it only in those who are ready to do whatever God may ask of them, no matter how hard or painful it may be. They are the ones whom "neither death, nor life, nor angels, nor principalities, nor powers, nor

[59] John 14:23.
[60] Matt. 7:21.

things present, nor things to come, nor might, nor height, nor depth, nor any other creature" can separate from "the love of God, which is in Christ Jesus our Lord."[61]

What, then, are we to think of Christ's love for us when measured by the same test? It was to help us that He went deliberately into the loneliness of the desert to endure hunger in His body and affliction in His soul; for neither hunger, nor the weariness of long watching, nor indignity, nor the assaults of evil, nor the agony of temptation could separate Him from His love of His fellowmen. It is that love, in all its greatness and intensity, which asks of us a like response.

Christ's assailant is referred to in the Gospels as "the Devil," "the tempter," and "Satan."[62] The name Satan is derived from the Hebrew verb *satan*, to oppose, and has therefore the general meaning of adversary. Occasionally in the Old Testament it is used of adversaries other than the Devil, but in various places, it is used as a proper name for the Devil,[63] and this usage is common in the New Testament.

Adversary describes the chief of the fallen angels in his relationship to the kingdom of God and to ourselves: he is the leader of the host of spirits who work to seduce us from our allegiance to God.

The term *devil*, on the other hand, is derived from the way in which the evil spirit goes about his work: it comes from the

[61] Rom. 8:38-39.
[62] Luke 4:2; Matt. 4:3; Mark 1:13.
[63] 1 Paralip. 21:1 (RSV = 1 Chron. 21:1); Zech. 3:1, 2; Job 1 and 2.

Greek noun *diabolos* which is, in turn, derived from the verb *diaballo*, to twist awry, to accuse, to calumniate. The noun is used in the general sense of calumniator by profane authors; in the New Testament, it is usually reserved for the prince of calumniators, who speaks evil of men to God and of God to men. It has thus the force of a personal title, although this is lost in English, where we use the word as a common noun to designate lesser evil spirits or demons as well as their leader.

There is food for thought in this derivation: it makes us see the peculiarly odious character of the sin of calumny, and shows us in what company we must be counted when we are guilty of it or of the closely related sin of detraction. When St. Paul chose the word *diabolos*, used elsewhere in the New Testament only of Satan, to qualify those guilty of these sins, he was no doubt concerned precisely to underline their diabolical character.[64]

More to our present purpose is the light the name throws on Satan's methods of procedure. He is the great calumniator because his purpose is to defame both God and man: to make God think ill of us and to make us think ill of God. He strove to defame man when he spoke to God of Job, portraying him as little better than a hypocrite, faithful only because it was in his own interest to be so.[65]

More often, and with better success, it is God whom he seeks to defame. So he persuaded Eve in the garden that God had forbidden them the fruit of the tree out of jealousy, lest they, too, should become as gods, and that He could not or

---

[64] 1 Tim. 3; 2 Tim. 3:3.
[65] Job 1:9-11.

would not punish their disobedience as He had threatened.[66] The method has served him well ever since. And he uses it again and again as he seeks to persuade us that God is unkind or unjust, and that it is only right that we should adjust the inequities of Providence in our regard or, at least, that if we do, we shall not suffer for it.

It is this same weapon of deceit that Satan turns against our Lord. In the first temptation, he points out the suffering that comes of serving God: what recompense is there for zeal and obedience but the pangs of hunger? In the second, he distorts the divine reality by suggesting that God is something to be used as a means, a sort of attendant spirit whom we can depend upon to do our bidding, to save us from harm if we court catastrophe: He will intervene, the suggestion is, whether you serve Him or not. The final defamation is the most audacious; for here he implies that God is unkind, ungrateful, and pays no heed to all Christ's service, while he, the Prince of this world, knows how to reward his servants.

We know Satan, then, as a malicious liar and deceiver. What else does revelation tell us of him? First, he is no mere personified abstraction: the Scriptures always present him as a real being, a mighty spirit, a great intelligence, inflexibly given over to evil. On the other hand, as we have seen, he is not the independent principle of evil whom the dualist religions of the East imagine to be in conflict with the principle of good on more or less equal terms: he is God's creature, originally the highest of angels, called like all the angels to eternal joy in God. But the joy was not forced on him: it was to be won by

[66] Gen. 3:1-5.

The Devil

the exercise, under grace, of his own freedom; it was his to choose, and, in fact, he chose otherwise. Instead of standing in the truth in which he had been created,[67] he deliberately abandoned it, impelled, it would seem, by pride;[68] and with him, there fell away a great number of the angels.[69] Thus, by their own choice, they were eternally excluded from Heaven and bound forever to the evil they had chosen.[70] Their rebellion stripped them of all their supernatural life and power; but their natural powers and activities remained to them, and these are henceforth devoted to expressing their pride and their enmity.

In the creation of man, Satan saw an opportunity of advancing his kingdom; and he would seem to have been spurred on by a special hatred, born of jealousy, for the human race. So he set out to subjugate humanity; he attacked the first human beings in the garden of Eden, and his attack succeeded. He established a sort of sovereignty over mankind, the reality of which our Lord Himself recognized. He held humanity in bondage and could therefore with truth be called the Prince of this world.[71]

It was Christ's mission to dispossess the Devil, to establish the kingdom of God in place of the kingdom of darkness and evil. The two are contrasting realities; and unless we really appreciate the horror of Satan's yoke, we can never have a

[67] John 8:44.
[68] 1 Tim. 3:6.
[69] Rev. 12:4.
[70] 2 Peter 2:4.
[71] John 12:31, 14:30, 16:11.

proper understanding of the deliverance which came to us through Christ.

After the initial victory, it was not necessary for Satan to appear openly, and, in fact, he preferred his activities to be hidden, although here and there in the Old Testament the veil is drawn aside for a moment lest we forget the fact that he is the source of all the corruption in which the world was steeped.[72] But the threat to his dominion presented by our Lord causes him to come once again into the open; and thus we are shown clearly what adversary the Word took flesh to overcome.

Against this background we can understand clearly the conflict on which our Lord was entering, and which was to take Him in the end to the Cross on Golgotha. This was to be no struggle against a blind, impersonal force such as we have in mind when we speak of man's struggle against the inimical forces of nature: it was to be a struggle against a personal enemy, purposeful, mighty, and wholly malicious — an enemy who, if defeated at one point, would return with greater fury to strike again from another.

This should sharpen our awareness of the struggle which faces us in our turn. In this initial engagement, Satan was overcome; he was overcome yet more thoroughly when he renewed his attack through the agency of the men whom he inspired to kill our Lord. But he did not give up the struggle. The foundations of the kingdom of God were laid; but that kingdom did not wholly displace the dominion of Satan in the

---

[72] Cf. 1 Paralip. 21:1 (RSV = 1 Chron. 21:1); 3 Kings 21:13 (RSV = 1 Kings 21:13).

world. The struggle still goes on; the Devil still "goes about," as we are told, "like a raging lion seeking whom he may devour,"[73] desiring to "sift us as wheat upon the threshing floor,"[74] and sometimes transforming himself into "an angel of light"[75] to achieve his ends.

∞

When Jesus was baptized, we are told, a voice from Heaven proclaimed: "This is my beloved Son in whom I am well pleased,"[76] and thereupon Jesus "returned from the Jordan full of the Holy Spirit, and was led by the Spirit into the desert."[77] The voice and the manifestation of the Spirit's presence at the baptism proclaim that this is the Promised One; they also inaugurate His messianic work. "The Lord had anointed Him, and the Spirit of the Lord was upon Him";[78] and by the Spirit He was led into the desert.

The role of the Spirit in the temptations is neither accidental nor irrelevant, and is stressed by all three synoptists. The two things, being God's Son and being led by His Spirit, go together; as St. Paul tells us, "Whosoever are led by the Spirit of God, they are the sons of God."[79] So the proclamation of our Lord's divine Sonship is followed at once by a striking submission to the leading of the Spirit.

[73] 1 Peter 5:8.
[74] Luke 22:31.
[75] 2 Cor. 11:14.
[76] Matt. 3:17.
[77] Luke 4:1.
[78] Cf. Isa. 61:1.
[79] Rom. 8:14.

It is followed *at once:* St. Mark tells us that Jesus went forthwith into the desert, immediately after His baptism.[80] We might well contrast with this our own behavior: we can be swift enough to act, and are indeed often headstrong and impulsive, where our pleasure or comfort is concerned; we are more likely to be sluggish and reluctant when it is a question of obeying the promptings of the Spirit.

But there is another lesson for us in the swiftness with which the Holy Spirit acted. The Spirit dwells in the soul as a principle of energy, of action: He comes to arouse the soul, to kindle a fire in it, to spur it forward. Through the sacraments, we are given divine life: the sacraments of the dead[81] make us sons of God, children by adoption of the heavenly Father; the other sacraments strengthen our title to that sonship. But the sonship is not given as just an honorary thing; it involves a real sharing in the life and activity of the Family into which we have been admitted. And as the divine life is given to us and strengthened in us, so the Spirit is present and active within us, to lead us forward to the activity proper to God's children — and to lead us, not in ways of our own choosing, but according as we are led.

The more fully a man is given to God, the more truly will the Spirit be his leader, and the less he will think of himself as being at his own disposal. Our temptation is to think of ourselves as self-sufficient, in no need of a guide; then we find ourselves driven remorselessly by desires and fears, and unable

---

[80] Mark 1:12.

[81] Sacraments given to those spiritually dead in sin, i.e., Baptism, Penance, and sometimes, Anointing of the Sick.

to reach the goals we have set ourselves. The lovers of God know and confess their insufficiency; but they have the peace and security which come of the knowledge that they are the sons of God and are therefore led along sure paths by His Spirit, and His rod and His staff are their comfort.[82]

Generally speaking, when the Scriptures tell us of the activity of the Spirit, He is shown as stirring mind and will to some great or heroic action. So it is here, when Jesus is led into the desert; so it was on the first Pentecost, when the coming of the Spirit sent the Apostles forth to preach the wonderful works of God.[83] But the Spirit is given, not just to a chosen few, but to all who are admitted to God's friendship. We are all given drink at a single source, the one Spirit.[84] St. Thomas expresses the common teaching of the Fathers and Doctors of the Church when he tells us that the operation of the Spirit, through His gifts, is necessary to us for our salvation.[85] So, in some way, the Spirit must come upon even the lowliest of those to whom grace is given, and the power of the Most High must overshadow them.

Only faith can discern this touch of glory which ennobles every Christian life. But the Spirit works so subtly that, generally speaking, even faith is blind to His presence and action: the soul is led without being aware of it. His manifest comings, as at the baptism of Christ or the first Pentecost, are the exception; normally, like the "spirit" or "breath" from which

[82] Ps. 22:3-4 (RSV = Ps. 23:3-4).
[83] Acts 2:4.
[84] 1 Cor. 12:13.
[85] *Summa Theologica*, I-II, Q. 68, art. 2.

He is named, He is seen not in Himself but in His effects. The leaves of the tree move, and we know it is the breath of the wind that moves them; the wind itself we do not see. "If He comes to me," said Job, "I shall not see Him; if He departs I shall not understand."[86]

Is there anything in ourselves to which we can point as proof of the Spirit's presence and activity within us? Can we say that we have risen to heights worthy of His leadership; or are we still groping dully about on the plains, our energies at best taken up with the struggle against the lure of sinful pleasures or laziness, against difficulties and failures in prayer, against weariness and boredom in our efforts to do good? If we seem to be in this latter case, it may be that we have failed to take the necessary steps to increase and intensify the workings of the Spirit within us. We are not to suppose that because we have received the Spirit in some small degree, we can therefore rest content: St. Luke tells us that Jesus went into the desert *filled* with the Spirit, and we, too, from no matter how great a distance, have to aspire to a similar fullness of life and of power.

An increase of that divine life and power comes to us through the sacraments, through prayer, and through good deeds. Perhaps, then, we are careless in our use of the sacraments, neglectful of prayer, or lacking in the zeal and energy to attempt to live a really good life. If so, we not only prevent any increase within us of the activity of the Spirit: we fail to respond to the impulse, the leading, which are already there. The failure, then, is ours: we have the gifts, but we fail to use

[86] Job 9:11.

them. We are like the servant in the parable who buried his talent in a napkin instead of making good use of it.[87]

But even those in whom there is no lack of good will, no serious failure to respond to God's grace, may still feel unhappy about what they regard as their lack of progress: instead of rising to great mystical heights, great spiritual achievements, they find themselves still pursuing very ordinary courses, always engaged in what may seem to be very humdrum or trivial or even ignoble tasks in the spiritual life. And then they may imagine that if only the Spirit would help them more vigorously, if only they had this or that grace, they would quickly rise to the heights of holiness.

It is at such times that the thought of Jesus being led into the desert to be tempted can be of great value. For, indeed, what destination or purpose could be more unlikely? Yet it was the Spirit that led Him.

The virtue of patience includes the ability to be patient with oneself, with one's own slowness and lack of apparent progress, and with one's own very pedestrian achievements. What we have to learn is simply to do the best we can and leave the results, our rate of progress, the direction in which we develop, in God's hands. When we seem to be doing what God wants of us and yet find ourselves weighed down by weakness, failure, temptation, or aridity, we can remember that it is God's way to ask unlikely or difficult things of us. We are here to glorify Him in ways not of our choosing but of His.

Our Lord could have dismissed the Devil with a word, but instead He chose willingly to be led by the Spirit to endure His

[87] Luke 19:20.

trial. This is the lesson St. Paul learned so well; he came to glory in his infirmities since, because of them, the power of Christ dwelt in him.[88] And St. James tells us to count it all joy when we encounter trials of every sort, knowing that the trying of our faith works patience.[89]

We have to be patient with God just as we have to be patient with ourselves. If, longing and praying for some grace, we become impatient and grumble because our prayers are not quickly heard, we might remember the words of Isaiah, "He that believeth, let him not hasten":[90] let him wait in patience for the time appointed by God. All that we have to do is prepare as best we can for the Spirit's coming, to be ready then to be led wherever He may will.

The Spirit is "breath," "wind," the mighty wind of the first Pentecost:[91] you think of a sailing ship becalmed until the wind rises; then the sails are filled, and the ship sweeps on. We have to be prepared simply to receive the wind when it comes; and we prepare by trying to grow in the gifts and fruits of the Spirit. If we do that, we need fear no trial or temptation, for we are under His leadership.

But His leadership does not annul our limitations. Our Lord tells us, "Be ye perfect";[92] but there is a world of difference between trying to be perfect and being a perfectionist, and an immense amount of harm is caused by confusing the two.

[88] 2 Cor. 12:9.
[89] James 1:2-3.
[90] Isa. 28:16.
[91] Acts 2:2.
[92] Matt. 5:48.

The Devil

Trying to be perfect means trying to make the best possible use of the gifts, natural and supernatural, which God has given us; and that, in turn, means being aware of, and accepting, our physical, psychological, and spiritual limitations. Being a perfectionist means fretting at those limitations, refusing to accept them, eating one's heart out because one cannot be something which, in fact, is out of one's range. The perfectionist may be highly talented, but he will be dissatisfied with his talents and perhaps come to hate them if they do not take him to the top of the tree. He may be a good painter or sculptor or singer, but he will be angry with himself and with fate and perhaps refuse to use his gifts at all if he finds he cannot be a Leonardo da Vinci, a Michelangelo, or an Enrico Caruso. So, instead of giving himself and others the joy his gifts could have brought him, he becomes frustrated and embittered.

It is the same in the spiritual life. God gives His grace in greater measure to some than to others. Trying to be perfect means trying to do *your* particular best, with the particular graces God has given *you*. You cannot pray like St. Teresa, any more than you can sing like Caruso: but how foolish if, for that reason, you give up trying to pray at all. What God asks of you is that you should do your best, not St. Teresa's best.

But the root of perfectionism is a perhaps unconscious pride which will not allow the ego to accept its limitations. And in the moral life, the ego's dark broodings over its unalterable shortcomings may easily be mistaken for sorrow for sin or that divine discontent which spurs the soul on to great spiritual achievement, and quite false moral standards may be set up as a result. The trouble is often intensified, if not begun, by foolish admonitions and counsels: "Just try harder, make more effort, and you'll be a great mystic like St. Teresa. Just pull yourself together, pray, and go regularly to the sacraments, and the most deeply ingrained bad habit will disappear."

To say things like that is not only stupid; it can be terribly harmful. Either the ego will be momentarily inflated with the thought that the limitations can be overcome after all, only to sink deeper into gloom when it becomes apparent that this is not true; or else the unfortunate person so admonished, knowing by bitter experience that the advice is not true, may be so discouraged as to give up the struggle altogether. Some kinds of compulsive habitual failings have to be treated as psychological rather than moral issues; and intense concentration on them, and tremendous attempts to conquer them by willpower, will only make things worse.

Again, the continuance of small temperamental failings is quite compatible with great growth in the love of God, compatible indeed with holiness; and if they prove ineradicable despite long years of arduous struggle, they must simply be numbered among the shortcomings which have to be accepted with good grace. It is tragic folly to concentrate on trying to be what one cannot be, and so to have no time or energy to give to the real task of trying to become what one can be.

"Be not solicitous," our Lord said.[93] You are to work, to struggle, to pray, but not to fret because you are what you are: your heavenly Father has care of you, in this as in all other matters; you, then, are to accept what you are, and to trust in Him. The moral perfectionist might remember the words of the psalmist, "*Elegi abjectus esse,*" I have chosen to be an

---

[93] Matt. 6:25.

outcast in the house of my God:[94] he has not been called to be a John of the Cross[95] or a Teresa of Avila,[96] but something much more lowly — and holy is God's name.

To be led by the Spirit, to be docile to His leadership, is to be led according to the measure of our God-given strength; it is not to be immune from trial and temptation. For the perfectionist, a temptation is an affront: he is hurt and bewildered by it, for he cannot fit it into his self-made ego-pattern. If, on the other hand, you are simply and humbly trying to do your best with your individual capacities, and are fully aware of your own limitations, temptation will come as no surprise: it will indeed be for you an honor if you feel that the Spirit is leading you into trials as He led our Lord.

And having led you there, He will not leave you helpless. For He is the Spirit who not only leads but comforts — strengthens — as well. The true meaning of *comfort* is indeed "to strengthen": not a soft, sentimental attempt to persuade us that all is well when all is far from well, but an attempt to pour into us new strength and courage to meet whatever demands are to be made on us. If, then, we are perplexed and hesitant, the Spirit enlightens us; if we are ignorant, He teaches us; if we are forgetful, He reminds us; and when we are weary and discouraged, He puts new heart into us. Whatever the trials to which He leads us, He is there to strengthen us, and to go with us through the ordeal to the end.

[94] Cf. Ps. 83:11 (RSV = Ps. 84:10).

[95] St. John of the Cross (1542-1591), mystic and Doctor of the Church.

[96] St. Teresa of Avila (1515-1582), Spanish Carmelite nun, mystic, and Doctor of the Church.

Chapter Three

The Desert: Glory and Crisis

It was immediately after His baptism that Jesus went into the desert to be tempted. It seems to be a general rule that times of great spiritual privilege or exaltation are followed by great temptations or spiritual crises: our Lord, then, who wished to be tried in all things as we are except sin, made Himself like us in this also. He warns us thereby that the reception of great graces, and particularly a call to some special role in the work of redemption, will bring great spiritual conflict in its wake. He exemplifies the wise counsel given of old by the son of Sirach: "Son, when thou comest to the service of God, stand in justice and in fear, and prepare thy soul for temptation."[97] Later, He was to reinforce the same lesson when He told the disciples who asked places at His right hand and His left: "You know not what you ask. Can you drink of the chalice that I drink of, or be baptized with the baptism wherewith I am baptized?"[98]

[97] Ecclus. 2:1.
[98] Mark 10:38.

The Devil

One reason for this close connection between glory and crisis lies, of course, in Satan's jealousy and hatred of anything which threatens his dominion. The very pronouncement from Heaven that God was pleased with His Son was certain to provoke Satan to attack Him if God allowed it; and so, as God did in fact allow it, Jesus must go from His baptism of water to a baptism of fire. In the same way, we are to think of Satan as filled with a special hatred of anyone favored by God, especially if that person is to be a powerful instrument for God's redemptive purposes in the world.

Again, Satan would be likely to choose such a time for his attacks because he knows that a man is likely to be especially vulnerable after being raised to new spiritual heights. For when a soul is thus raised up, it undergoes a sort of moral conversion: it aspires to a greater perfection than before; the old ways will not do, will not respond to the new ideals. And for a time, it may not be difficult to live up to these new ideals: a lingering sense of exaltation may make it easy. But only for a time: the building up of the virtues and qualities which will make it an easy and spontaneous thing to live at this higher level has not yet been achieved; and so it happens that when the mood of exaltation wears off, as it soon must, the soul begins to feel the real difficulty of what is being attempted. This, then, is the critical stage, when the soul is very vulnerable; and it is at this moment that Satan is likely to strike.

So it was with our Lord. St. Mark and St. Luke do not determine exactly the precise moment of Satan's attack: we could understand them as meaning that the temptations lasted through the forty days. But St. Matthew clearly places them at the end, and most commentators are agreed that the assault came only after the forty days of fasting. Satan is a good psychologist: he knew that this was the moment best suited to his purposes. Jesus, we are to suppose, had come from the Jordan, from the proclamation of His Father's joy in Him, in an ecstatic exaltation of soul, "filled with the Holy Spirit." He had undertaken a stupendous fast combined with long hours of watching and praying. Now, when He was faint from hunger, when His exalted mood seemed to be leaving Him, was the time when Satan could best hope to find a weakness in Him.

We, for our part, are well advised to expect that chilling of mood which is sure to follow, sooner or later, on any heightening of fervor; for if we fail to anticipate it and to make intelligent provision against the temptations which are sure to come, we may well have little to show for our confessions, prayers, retreats, and other times of spiritual renewal. We may be sincere enough at the time; there may be no doubt of our good intentions. But the fact that we fail to look ahead to the time of aridity, when everything will seem boring and insipid, means that when the time comes, it will take us by surprise, we shall have no defenses prepared, and so we shall be an easy prey to temptation.

When, therefore, we are moved by God's grace to try to make something better than before out of our lives, common sense demands that we should have in mind the difficulties which lie ahead. In the fervor of the moment, what we are attempting may seem easy; but we must not be deceived: it is not easy. If we are wise, we shall think out well in advance what to do when our efforts begin to be labored and elation is succeeded by depression and discouragement.

The Devil

But the Devil's eagerness to attack us, and our own vulnerability, will account for temptation only if it is assumed that God allows us to be tempted; and this assumption may well seem out of keeping with our idea of His love and mercy, of His concern for all His creatures, particularly those to whom He gives special graces. So, when St. Thomas, who, in any case, was usually chiefly concerned to explain things in relation to their First Cause, asks why it is that temptation follows on the reception of grace, he is content to find reasons why God should allow this to be so. And he offers five reasons why this permission, far from showing a lack of divine love, is, on the contrary, a proof of it and of God's desire to enrich the soul.[99]

The first reason is that temptation *tests* the virtue of the just. That God does, in fact, so prove the just is made very clear in the Bible. Abraham's faith was tested;[100] the manna given to the Chosen People was to show whether or not they would walk in God's law;[101] their wanderings, too, were to manifest what was in their hearts, whether they would keep the commandments or not.[102] Moses told his people, "The Lord your God trieth you, that it may appear whether you love Him with all your heart and with all your soul or not."[103] And this appears to be the lot of all the just, for we read of them that God has tried them and found them worthy of Himself.[104]

---

[99] *Commentary on Matthew*, ch. 4.
[100] Gen. 22:1-12; cf. Heb. 11:17.
[101] Exod. 16:4.
[102] Deut. 8:2.
[103] Deut. 13:3.
[104] Wisd. 3:5.

Now, the purpose of the trial is certainly not to show God the true disposition of the soul: that He already knows. It must, then, be for the enlightenment of the man tempted, and perhaps of others also. Man is largely a mystery to himself. He does not know what he can endure and what he cannot. Sometimes he will be rash, and attempt things far beyond his strength; at other times, he will fall easily into despair, imagining himself unequal to something which is well within his powers. "What doth he know, who hath not been tried?" asks Ecclesiasticus:[105] it is only when temptation comes to search him that he discovers himself.

So it was that Peter rashly declared himself ready to go with Jesus to prison and to death.[106] Our Lord knew his weakness, and warned him; but Peter had to learn his own lesson. It took the temptation and the fall and then the tears to teach him where his strength lay: once he had learned that, the power he lacked was given to him, so that thereafter his faith failed not.

We are in a like case. We are so blind to our real needs that we do not even know what we ought to pray for;[107] nor do we recognize the blessings for which we should give thanks to God. And, as St. Augustine was so fond of asking, how shall we know unless God teach us, as He taught Peter, by letting our hearts be searched by trial?[108]

---

[105] Ecclus. 34:9.

[106] Luke 22:33.

[107] Rom. 8:26.

[108] This theme is a favorite one with St. Augustine; let it suffice to cite these two of the many passages in which he dwells upon it: Exposition on Ps. 36:1, *Patrologia Latina* 36, col. 355; Exposition on Ps. 55, *Patrologia Latina* 36, col. 647, 648.

The Devil

The second reason God allows men to be tempted is to check their ruinous tendency to pride, which can make even God's goodness to them an occasion of sin. Temptation will remind them of their own weakness, and their dependence on God. This was true even of St. Paul, who tells us, "Lest the greatness of the revelations should exalt me, there was given me a sting in my flesh, an angel of Satan, to buffet me."[109]

Thirdly, temptation may be permitted for the discomfiture of the devils, to show them their powerlessness against the grace of Christ. In the book of Job, we read that God said to Satan, "Hast thou considered my servant Job, that there is none like him in the earth, a simple and upright man, and fearing God and avoiding evil?"[110] Similarly, St. Thomas suggested, the just man may be exposed to trial for the confusion of the powers of evil, as though God should say to them, "Consider this servant of mine, and know that against him you can accomplish nothing."

Fourthly, temptation can serve to harden and strengthen the man who is tried by it. The nations that were left by Joshua, when he died, were not destroyed: God suffered them to remain "that by them He might instruct Israel, and all that had not known the wars of the Canaanites; that afterward their children might learn to fight with their enemies, and to be trained up to war."[111] Nothing is more enervating than prolonged inactivity. A man's capacities will grow when demands are put upon him which tax his energies and call forth

[109] 2 Cor. 12:7.
[110] Job 1:8.
[111] Judg. 3:1-2.

his strongest efforts, for, generally speaking, he will be likely to exert himself only as far as he must. The same sort of thing is likely to happen in the soul when no demands are made of it; and for that reason, the absence of temptation can in some circumstances be a greater danger than temptation itself.

Lastly, St. Thomas tells us, God allows the just to be tempted to show them the greatness which grace bestows on them. It is an honor to be attacked by the Devil. Behemoth, we read, disdains to drink at any mere puddle of water, trusting that "the Jordan may run into his mouth."[112] And Satan likewise will not bother with prey unworthy of his efforts. So God gives the just the consolation of knowing they are of sufficient worth to have aroused the anger of the Devil; just as at other times He would perhaps give us subtle warning by letting us go on long untroubled.

Jesus was led into the "desert." This was evidently the wild tract of country west of the Jordan: a bare, rugged range of hills extending from north to south, scarred with innumerable ravines cut by the torrents which at times pour down the hillsides; beyond these, a great expanse of sandy hills, barren and desolate. The word used by St. Matthew to tell of our Lord being led by the Spirit suggests that He was led upward, so that some writers take this as indicating that he was taken to some high point in the hills.[113]

The exact location, however, is unimportant; for the evangelists, it is simply "the desert"; the significant facts for us to

---

[112] Job 40:18.

[113] Cf. Louis-Claude Fillion, *La Vie de Notre Seigneur Jesus-Christ; exposé historique, critique et apologétique* (Paris: Librairie Letouzey et Ane, 1925), vol. 1, 54.

dwell on are that it was a desolate and solitary place — St. Mark underlines its loneliness when he tells us that Jesus was "with beasts"[114] — and that the trial probably took place in a high place. So Moses went up to the solitude of the mountain-top before receiving the Law from God's hands;[115] so John the Baptist lived his early life in the wilderness as a preparation for his ministry.[116] Jesus, then, chose to follow the example of Moses, who prefigured him, and of John, His precursor.

But, indeed, innumerable holy people have followed the same path, have retired in one way or another to a desert place, to solitude, in order to seek God — and, perhaps, themselves. Antony[117] and his disciples fled the noise and turmoil and vice of Alexandria to seek God in the Egyptian desert; and Benedict[118] lived alone in his cave before he set about his great monastic undertaking. The period of quiet thought precedes the outburst of activity, because only so can the activity be thoughtful — and perhaps in the long run, as much damage is done in the world by thoughtless action as by deliberate malice. And quiet thought is easier to achieve in silence and solitude than in the noise and confusion of a big city.

We tend nowadays to be afraid of silence and solitude and stillness: we seek the protection of the ceaselessly blaring radio, of incessant chatter; we must always be on the move. And perhaps it is precisely thought that we are escaping from.

[114] Mark 1:13.
[115] Exod. 24:18.
[116] Luke 1:80.
[117] St. Antony (c. 251-356), "The Abbot," patriarch of all monks.
[118] St. Benedict of Nursia (c. 480-550), the patriarch of Western monasticism.

The Desert: Glory and Crisis

In the Christian tradition, silence is a good thing, to be sought after, and noise a privation of it; stillness is a good thing, and excessive or purposeless activity a privation of it; solitude is a good thing, at least sometimes, for if we are always talking to other people, we shall find it hard ever to talk to God. When Elijah sought God, he found Him, not in the sound and fury of mighty wind and fire and earthquake, but in the "still, small voice":[119] we shall not hear that if we are not quiet ourselves.

The Israelites, after that passage through the Red Sea, which was a prefiguring of Baptism, spent many years in the wilderness before reaching the Promised Land. The baptized Christian is well advised to follow the same pattern: either literally or metaphorically to seek or fashion for himself a solitude where he can hear God's voice. "I will lead her into the wilderness," writes the prophet Hosea, "and I will speak to her heart."[120]

The desert, in one sense or another, is a necessary condition of spiritual development. For most of us, the greater part of life is inevitably occupied with immediate concerns at a more or less shallow level: the everyday routine tasks, the demands of social life, and the endless superficial calls on our attention and time and energies. In all this bustle of mind, if not of body, generous impulses and stirrings of thought or feeling which could lead to better and deeper things are easily lost sight of and forgotten. Hence the need to withdraw at times to a "desert place apart"[121] where we can attempt to live

---

[119] 3 Kings 19:12 (RSV = 1 Kings 19:12).
[120] Hos. 2:14.
[121] Matt. 14:13; Mark 6:32; Luke 4:42.

The Devil

at a deeper level, to be aware of the hidden things — above all
of the hidden Presence. So when the cock crew and made
Peter aware of his betrayal, he "went out and wept bit-
terly":[122] being alone was a help to his repentance and his
sorrow, and so led to the deepening of his understanding, faith,
and love.

It is one thing to be afraid of solitude; it is quite another to
recoil from loneliness: as we have seen, even our Lord did that.
But perhaps sometimes, if we find ourselves afflicted with
loneliness, we might do well to think of it as God's attempt to
give us — to force on us — a solitude we should not bother, or
wish, to achieve for ourselves. If at least we take it in that way,
and turn to God instead of bemoaning our lack of human
companionship, it may be that great things will be done in us
which we would otherwise, in the clatter of human conversa-
tion, have been incapable of receiving.

Many men know moments of crisis, of challenge, which
they can only face and think out alone; and there are times
when God seems to strip His servants of all their resources,
even the help and guidance of their friends, so that they may
rely for once only on Him. Here, too, our Lord has gone before
us: the solitude of the desert underlines for us the fact that He
stood alone and friendless in this first critical moment; later,
in the supreme crisis of the agony in the garden, His sleeping
disciples make Him equally friendless, bereft;[123] in both cases,
"it was His alone to tread the winepress."[124]

[122] Luke 22:62.
[123] Matt. 26:40; Mark 14:37.
[124] Cf. Isa. 63:3.

Now, "Jesus was led . . . to be tempted": as we have already seen, it is as though He would actually invite — provoke — the temptation; and this suggestion is enforced by the fact that it is to the desert that the Holy Spirit leads Him, and that, as St. Mark says, He was "with beasts." For a very old tradition, going back to Babylonia and Assyria, makes the wild and desert places, the "wastelands," the abode of wild beasts and demons.[125] When Isaiah depicts Edom in ruins, he describes how "thorns and nettles shall grow in its palaces, briers over its battlements; it shall be the lair of serpents. . . . Devils and monstrous forms shall haunt it, satyr call out to satyr; there the vampire lies down and finds rest."[126] And when he foretells the doom of Babylon, it is in similar terms: "Wild beasts will make their lairs in it; its houses will be tenanted by serpents; ostriches will nest there, and satyrs dance; the owls will hoot to one another in its palaces, birds of ill omen in its temples of delight."[127]

There may be some connection between these satyrs, or "hairy ones," and the animal-deities to whom the Israelites sacrificed in imitation of the Egyptians, and we have already noted how the goat is the object of adoration in the medieval sabbats; we may recall, too, how in the Second Coming, the sheep are to be divided from the goats, a thought resumed in the *Dies Irae: Et ab haedis me sequestra; statuens in parte dextra.*[128]

---

[125] So also the unclean spirit which has gone out of a man "walks about the desert looking for a resting place" (Matt. 12:43; Knox).

[126] Isa. 34:13-14 (Knox).

[127] Isa. 13:21-22 (Knox).

[128] "And from the goats afar divide me; to Thy right hand do Thou guide me"; cf. Matt. 25:32-33.

The Devil

The satyrs, then, are symbols of evil — some versions call them simply "demons" — just as the wildernesses are symbols of carnage, lamentation, and desolation. To go into the wilderness, therefore, is to risk, or invite, a meeting with evil spirits; and this is what our Lord does.

But to invite such a meeting might well seem to us unlawful; it goes against what we are apt to assume to be the only prudent attitude to temptation: have we not been taught from childhood to "flee every occasion of sin"? Indeed, we tend easily enough to think of all our troubles, temptations among them, as due to some external cause, and so to try to escape them by running away from them. And sometimes, of course, we are right; troubles do come upon us which are none of our making; and sometimes, therefore, the right and sensible thing is to run away. This is as true of temptation as of other misfortunes. So when the angels led Lot and his family out of the doomed city and put him on his way, they bade him not to linger but to flee for his life without once looking back.[129]

But flight is not always an effective remedy for temptation. If it is Satan with whom we are at issue, we shall not escape him by running away, for there is nowhere we can take sanctuary. Certainly the desert will not discourage him who goes about the waterless places looking for those who might have escaped him.[130]

But, in any case, fleeing would not, for the most part, save us, for we carry our tempter within ourselves. True, there are some temptations due to our own unruly impulses which are

[129] Gen. 19:17.
[130] Cf. Luke 11:24.

best met by a metaphorical flight. We may recall Baudouin's Law, that when the imagination and the will are in open conflict, the imagination always wins: if, by attempting a direct repudiation of the temptation, we merely cause it to loom larger and larger in the imagination, we are courting disaster; the only hope lies in trying to engage the imagination with other things.

But there are also occasions when to refuse to face a temptation is merely a sign of laziness or cowardice or procrastination: an issue is involved about which sooner or later we shall have to reach a decision, and the longer we refuse to face the issue, the longer it will haunt us and, in so doing, drain us of resources which could be put to better, more productive uses. There are times when we have to try to imitate the boldness of our Lord in going out to meet temptation.

Certainly that boldness can never be a justification for carelessness about avoiding occasions of sin. St. Thomas tells us that there are two kinds of temptation: one arises from the proximity of unnecessary and dangerous occasions of sin, and this should always be avoided; the other arises from the doing of good, for this is always calculated to rouse Satan to attack. Our Lord's temptation was of this kind; and here we are certainly right in trying to copy His boldness. So St. John Chrysostom remarks that it was not only Christ who was led by the Spirit into the desert, but that all the children of God who have the same Spirit are likewise led.[131]

For they are not content to sit in idleness: the Spirit drives them to the undertaking of great things. And this is to be in

[131] Cf. *Summa Theologica*, III, Q. 41, art. 2.

the desert, so far as the Devil is concerned, for in good works, there is none of the injustice in which he delights. And every good work is a desert also so far as the flesh and the world are concerned, for good works are barren of all that is according to the will of the flesh and the spirit of worldliness.

"And when He had fasted forty days and forty nights . . ."[132] We read that both Moses and Elijah endured fasts of the same length — Moses, to prepare himself to receive the Law; Elijah, as he walked to the mountain of God to hear the divine announcement that the Law was to be restored.[133] Our Lord would not prepare with any less solemnity for what lay before Him; nor would He do more, for He came in the form of a servant and would therefore be like His fellow servants.

Is there any special significance in this number forty? Nowadays, perhaps, we tend to be skeptical about the symbolism of numbers, to think it all very childish and unreal. Yet it has a long and interesting history, going far back into antiquity, so we ought to beware of dismissing it too lightly. Does not the Bible tell us, "Thou hast ordered all things in measure and number and weight"?[134]

It is certainly curious how often this number forty recurs in the Bible in contexts which all have common elements — often enough, it would seem, to lead us to suppose there must be mystery in it. There are the forty days of the Flood[135] and forty days in which the body of Jacob was kept embalmed

---

[132] Matt. 4:2.
[133] Deut. 9:9; 3 Kings 19:8 (RSV = 1 Kings 19:8).
[134] Wisd. 11:21.
[135] Gen. 7:12.

before burial.[136] The men sent out by Moses to view the land of Canaan were forty days on their mission;[137] and for forty days, Goliath, who typifies our adversary Satan, stood defying the children of Israel.[138] For forty years, the Hebrews wandered in the wilderness before reaching the Promised Land;[139] for forty days, Ezekiel was to sleep on his right side, taking on himself the iniquity of the house of Judah;[140] and for forty years, the cities of Egypt lay desolate.[141] Finally, it was for forty days that the risen Christ remained on earth before ascending to the Father.[142] The number suggests, then, a period of preparation for some renewal or fulfillment, and a preparation by way of prayer, solitude, hardship, and purification.

Some would see a further significance in the number as deriving from four and ten. Four is the symbol of matter, the created universe, and humanity, as opposed to three, which is spirit, divinity. There are the four elements (earth, air, fire, and water), the four seasons, the four points of the compass, the four phases of the moon, the four functions which together make up the complete human psyche; there are the four arms of the cross: in the Greek cross, with its four equal arms, humanity fulfilled and made perfect by grace; in the unequal Latin cross, with one arm plunging down into the earth, humanity still in travail, the work of redemption still incomplete.

[136] Gen. 50:3.
[137] Num. 13:26.
[138] 1 Kings 17:16 (RSV = 1 Sam. 17:16).
[139] Exod. 16:35.
[140] Ezek. 4:6.
[141] Cf. Ezek. 19:12.
[142] Acts 1:3.

The material creation reveals God the Tetragrammaton,[143] its Maker (as the four Gospels reveal the God of grace); at the same time, the number four suggests the square and the cube, for firmness and stability: *"Fundasti terram super stabilitatem suam,"* the psalmist tells us, "The earth Thou hast planted on its own firm base, undisturbed for all time."[144] For all its perpetual flux, the world — and humanity with it — derives stability and endurance from God, and in the soul of man, for all its superficial wanderings and shallow and shifting interests, there is the "still point," the "fund of the spirit" where God is found and felt.

The number ten is often used in the Bible simply to denote a round or complete number, as with the ten talents,[145] ten virgins,[146] ten lepers,[147] and so on. But you find it in more-exalted contexts: ten candlesticks adorn the sanctuary;[148] the Law is given in the form of ten commandments;[149] and the story of creation is given to us divided into ten moments, each beginning with the words "and God said."[150] We might recall also the tithes which figure so largely in the Old Law,[151] especially as the idea of paying tithes to God has been so much

---

[143] The technical term for the four-letter Hebrew name of God: YHWH or JHVH.

[144] Ps. 103:5 (RSV = Ps. 104:5).

[145] Luke 19:13.

[146] Matt. 25:1.

[147] Luke 17:12.

[148] 2 Paralip. 4:7 (RSV = 2 Chron. 4:7).

[149] Exod. 34:28.

[150] Gen. 1.

[151] Lev. 27:30.

associated in the Church's history with our own forty days of Lent, roughly one tenth of the year.

If, then, we put all these symbols together, we have a picture of humanity, still like the rest of creation in travail, needing to withdraw sometimes into solitude, to search for stillness in the hurly-burly of life, and to give at least a tithe of its time and attention to God; and needing also its recurrent purifications, its moments of renewal and rebirth, as an essential part of that arduous process whereby it is to come to its fulfillment, its completion, in the end.

Our Lord's fast, then, was a very long one, and it would seem to have been absolute. For St. Luke tells us definitely that throughout the forty days, Jesus ate nothing;[152] and while we are not told whether He abstained also from water, it seems probable, partly because we do know that this was true of the fast of Moses, and we should not expect our Lord's to be less severe, and partly because of the nature of the place: the arid, waterless desert. Such a fast is certainly an outstanding example of physical endurance, the more so as both Matthew and Luke seem to suggest that it was not until the end of the forty days that Jesus was "hungry"[153] — which presumably we are to interpret as meaning faint and weak from hunger.

Yet it would not seem to involve the miraculous: there are other examples of Christ's physical strength and endurance, as, for example, in some of His long journeyings through hilly country and in great heat or in His ability to do without sleep. Moreover, we find instances of remarkable insensibility to

---

[152] Luke 4:2.
[153] Matt. 4:2; Luke 4:2.

pain and other sense phenomena in times of intense concentration even in the cases of men in whom we should expect a far less perfect subordination of body to mind.

Why did our Lord endure this long and exhausting fast? In the immediate context, the most obvious reason was to provoke Satan to attack Him: as we have seen, it was in order to be tempted that He went into the desert. And the fast would be likely to incite Satan because, first of all, it was a good work, and not merely a good work but, seen in the obvious comparison with the fasts of Moses and Elijah, a momentous work and one of messianic significance: Satan would be on the alert to seize the first favorable moment for attack because he saw in the person of Christ a tremendous threat to his own kingdom. And this would be such a moment, because our Lord's physical weakness must weaken His resistance. The Devil is adept at thus choosing the most suitable moment. In our Lord's parable, it is while the farmer is asleep that his enemy comes and sows weeds among his wheat;[154] in the beginning of the story of mankind, it is while Eve is alone that the Devil tries his wiles on her.

There is a very practical moral for us here. Certain conditions of mind and body do, in fact, make us an easy prey to temptation, and we have to do what we prudently can to avoid them. In times of extreme bodily fatigue or mental tension, we are much more readily open to suggestion than when we are well and strong in body and tranquil in mind. That is why we are told never to undertake physical mortifications except under direction.

[154] Matt. 13:25.

We are to follow Christ into the desert, yes; but the imitation is not to be absolute. He had no need to be cautious for fear of taxing Himself beyond the limits of His resources; we have. It is a very misguided fervor that leads people to adopt penitential practices which undermine their health and therefore their ability to work for God. We have to be realistic: it is possible to be overcautious and (perhaps in obedience to an unacknowledged love of comfort and well-being) to underestimate our natural powers and the strength given us by grace; but it is also possible to overestimate them (perhaps in obedience to an unacknowledged pride or vanity) and to attempt imprudently more than we should, the *mirabilia super me* of the psalmist, the "wonderful matters beyond my strength."[155]

It remains true that our Lord's example is there to remind us of our need to arm ourselves against temptation by fasting and self-denial. That His own fast was meant to be an example for us has always been assumed by the Fathers of the Church; He Himself told us that there are some devils who are only to be driven out by prayer and fasting;[156] and the Church underlines our need of self-denying practices by Her yearly Lenten fast. Nowadays, it is true, modern conditions absolve very many from the duty of fasting as such; but there are other equivalent ways of exercising self-denial and so of achieving that discipline without which we should be powerless against temptation. For resistance to temptation means quelling powerful impulses; and this only the disciplined personality can do. If we are in the habit of giving way to every passing whim

---

[155] Cf. Ps. 138:6 (RSV = Ps. 139:6).
[156] Mark 9:28 (RSV = Mark 9:29).

and desire, we shall be in no position to exercise self-control in the moment of temptation.

We have, too, our Lord's express injunction that to be a Christian, a man must deny himself and take up his cross daily[157] — his cross, certainly, as measured by his individual capacities and God's will for him, but a cross nonetheless. Self-denial is an integral part of the Christian life, and we are to address ourselves to it seriously and systematically, and to correct the situation whenever we find ourselves becoming slack and soft; for negligence or indifference is bound to lead to spiritual weakness.

Christian writers have seen further significance in the sequence of baptism, fast, temptation. The fast follows immediately on the baptism: grace received from God should not be allowed to lie idle; the Christian is to attempt forthwith to make good use of it, to attempt to achieve something worthwhile. Thus, for instance, the *Ite, missa est*,[158] which announces the conclusion of the Sacrifice of the Mass, is not just a statement of fact, but a challenge. Go, in the power and the strength here given you, go back to the everyday world and help there in the work of bringing God to the world and the world to God.

The temptation, in its turn, follows immediately on the fast, to teach us how to arm ourselves against the assaults of evil. Our great defense is the grace of God, and it is freely given, but only if we sincerely desire it and show our desire in the ways appointed by God: prayer and the sacraments, on the

[157] Luke 9:23.
[158] "Go, you are dismissed."

one hand, but also a certain degree of austerity and self-denial on the other. Prayer and fasting go together: as we have seen, the forty days in the desert are the symbol of a search for God and for personal integrity made up of prayer, solitude, hardship, and purification. The prayer of the completely selfish and self-indulgent man would carry little weight, we are to suppose, for the desires it expressed could hardly be thought deep or sincere enough to make it fitting that God should satisfy them. *Ex animo contrito et humili corde:* we are to approach God, the Mass tells us, with humble and contrite hearts, not merely acknowledging our weaknesses and failures, but determined, with the help of His grace, to improve the situation, to be less selfish and more generous for the future.

Chapter Four

Stones or Bread?

"And the tempter came and said to Him, 'If Thou be the Son of God, command that these stones be made bread.' "[159]

If Satan is subtle in his choice of the opportune moment for attack, he is equally subtle in playing on the character, particular dispositions, needs, desires, and circumstances of his intended victim. And if the victim is a good man, the Devil will not court certain defeat by suggesting something wholly evil which would be rejected out of hand: *larvatus prodeo*, he will mask the evil under a show of good; he will set himself to disorganize the man's feelings and will about something which in itself is innocent and perhaps even praiseworthy. This is the case here with the first temptation: what more right and proper than that when a man is exhausted with hunger, he should eat?

Nonetheless for many centuries the ecclesiastical writers commonly regarded this incident as a temptation to gluttony;

[159] Matt. 4:3.

and we should not simply brush this view aside, as some modern authors do, as though it were naive and foolish. There is no gluttony, they argue, in wanting to appease extreme hunger when there is no obligation to fast any further,[160] and this is true enough, but it is not the whole story. Gluttony is not just a matter of overeating or of an excessive hankering after food; there are many ways, as the moralists point out, in which we can fail to keep our eating or our will to eat within reasonable bounds. We can sin by eating too much, but also by eating too voraciously, by keeping too sumptuous a table, by an excessive niceness about what we shall or shall not eat. And we can sin by eating *praepropere*: by being too precipitate, too impatient to wait for the proper time or manner. If we were so avid for food that we were prepared to resort to unreasonable means of obtaining it, that would be a sin of gluttony even if in the food itself there were nothing excessive in quantity or quality.

It is this question of means which is important here. Had Satan merely suggested that it would be a good thing for our Lord to eat, now that His fast was accomplished, there would have been nothing evil in the suggestion. What, in fact, he does is to urge our Lord to use His supernatural powers for this purpose, and this would have been wrong. It would have been wrong for two reasons.

First, as St. Thomas puts it, it is wrong to seek food for oneself by miraculous means when it can be obtained by ordinary human means.[161] Grace is not a substitute for nature;

---

[160] Cf. Ferdinand Prat, *Jesus Christ* (Milwaukee: Bruce, 1950), vol. 1, 156.

[161] *Summa Theologica*, III, Q. 41, art. 4.

it works in and through nature, healing and perfecting it and raising its activities to a higher plane. So, as St. Paul tells us, we are to give glory to God in all that we do, all the natural activities of everyday life, our eating and drinking, our work and our play.[162] For while they are natural, they are also engraced; they are part of our love of God and our obedience to His will for us. Nothing could be more misguided than to suppose that we may expect God to achieve for us by a miracle what we can perfectly well achieve for ourselves by a little hard work.

But our Lord was tempted to use not merely His supernatural but His messianic powers for His own purposes. These had been given to Him for the work He had to do in the world, for the good of humanity. He was not to use them for His own advantage: no legions of angels were to rescue Him from torture and death at the end, for it was to suffer torture and death that He came into the world.[163] Had He listened, then, to this second implication in Satan's words, He would have been false to the very essence of His mission: He would no longer have been the Messiah for whose coming the centuries had longed, the promised Shepherd who was to lay down His life for His sheep.[164]

"*If* Thou be," the tempter says. As we have seen, had he been certain of our Lord's divinity, he would not have tried to tempt Him; he knew that He was gifted with supernatural power, that He was perhaps the Messiah, certainly that He was

---

[162] 1 Cor. 10:31.
[163] Cf. Matt. 26:53; John 12:27.
[164] John 10:11.

a threat to the satanic kingdom if He used His powers according to the will of God. Some writers, then, have seen in this temptation an *exploratio divinitatis*, an attempt to discover just in what sense Jesus was the Son of God, whether He was not merely human but divine. But the purpose, or at least the main purpose, of a temptation is not to acquire information but to cause evil to be done; it seems wiser, then, to take the phrase "Son of God" in its wider sense as meaning simply one specially favored by God, and to see in the implied doubt, "If You really are that," an attempt to goad our Lord into the vanity of demonstrating His power.[165]

It is this idea of power misused which forms the essence of the threefold temptation as a whole. The power was His to use for the doing of good; it was good that He should satisfy His hunger; what, then, was wrong in Satan's suggestion? Simply that in obedience to His Father, the Word had taken on Himself the form of a servant:[166] it was not for Him, therefore, to satisfy His own human needs in superhuman ways.

St. Thomas speaks of the course suggested by the Devil as a *deordinatio*, a perversion of the proper order of things. Had our Lord adopted it, He would have been guilty of the very evil He had come to remedy, the essential evil which had been in man's Original Sin and thenceforth, in one way or another, in every subsequent evil act: the arrogant assumption that the satisfaction of one's own needs, desires, and ambitions is more important than doing the will of God. The apple in the garden

---

[165] Cf. Lagrange, *Evangile Selon Saint Matthieu*, 2nd ed. (Paris: J. Gabalda, 1923), 59.

[166] Phil. 2:7-8.

of Eden is the symbol of just that: Eve was lured into obeying a lust for godly self-aggrandizement instead of obeying God; had Jesus turned the stones into bread, He would have been doing the same thing. But no, as later He was to say that His food was to do the will of His Father,[167] so here He replies that to be truly alive, man needs more than bodily nourishment: he needs the nourishment of God's word, God's expressed will.

Lagrange points out the striking relevance of our Lord's quotation from Deuteronomy: the people of Israel had been hungry as He was hungry, and God had sent them manna to eat: He would have not done less for His Son (nor did He later on) had it been necessary. And our Lord's refusal to obey the Devil's suggestion was a refusal to try to force His Father's hand and equally a refusal to fail in His trust in God's care for Him. That the way of God's will was a hard way for Him He knew well enough, just as He knew that the way of Satan would be an easy one; nonetheless it is in God that we must trust, even — or rather, especially — in times of great trial and hardship. Bread will keep the body alive; but only that trust in God and the obedience which springs from it will give vitality to the soul.

From distrust it is a very short step to disobedience. So it was in the beginning, in the garden of Eden: if the fruit of the tree which would make them as gods has been forbidden them, so the serpent argues, it must be because God has no care for them — indeed, far from caring for their welfare, He is jealous of them. So it was again with the Hebrews when they were hungry in the desert and cried out for bread, and having none,

[167] John 4:34.

77

began to lose their trust in God until, in the end, they murmured against Him and complained that He had led them out into the desert only to die of famine.[168]

So here also it is Jesus' trust in His Father that Satan is seeking to undermine. As we have seen, the purpose of "If Thou be the Son of God" is not to gain information for himself about our Lord: it reflects, not a hesitation in his own mind, but one he would like to engender in the mind of Christ. Satan is saying in effect: "You heard the voice from Heaven telling You that You are God's beloved Son; and that is a wonderful thing, certainly, if it is true. But are You quite sure it is true? Can You really be God's beloved Son, considering the plight You are in? Would God, could God, allow His beloved Son to be reduced to such extremities of hardship and need? Did You perhaps take the voice too seriously? Could You be deluded? For the facts certainly suggest simply that You are a starving man who must quickly find a way to eat or else must perish."

We can readily see that Satan's argument was not a sound one, but it was specious. It is an argument of the type which will always appeal to those who think of natural blessings as unequivocal signs of God's favor; it might well prove effective even with a great man if his judgment were impaired by fatigue and hunger. Too easily we forget that good things, the objects of natural and legitimate desire, do not necessarily come in greatest abundance to the wisest and best of men; on the contrary, the good must often go hungry, suffer affliction, or pass through the trackless and waterless desert; but this does not mean that God, their Father, has no care for them.

[168] Cf. Exod. 16:3.

Stones or Bread?

The flaw in Satan's argument did not, as he had hoped, escape our Lord, who swiftly rebutted it, and equally swiftly rebuffed the appeal to His emotions which lay behind it: Satan was trying to make Him feel sorry for Himself. "Too much is being asked of You; and in the end, what does it all profit You? Hunger and weariness is all Your reward from God's hands. Had You not better find another patron — a patron who will take better care of You than that?" But our Lord had, not merely in His mind but in His heart, the truth expressed by the psalmist, who would choose rather to be an outcast in the house of his Lord than live luxuriously in the palaces of sinners.[169]

There is a great deal in all this that we can apply to our own lives. Christ was tempted to use His messianic powers to His own advantage: how often the same sort of thing happens among men! Those of us who are priests, for instance, are given power, authority, and influence in order to serve souls; but we can be tempted to abuse these things and pervert God's order by turning them to our own advantage, our own desire for self-aggrandizement of one sort or another. Instead of being true priests, we can degenerate into money-grubbers or petty tyrants, careerists or snobs; and so the assault of Satan which failed with our Lord will succeed in us: we shall be false to our office.

The same temptation can come to parents, who are given power and authority by God to be used for the good of their children. They can instead use that power to force their children to serve their own selfish ends. The possessive mother,

[169] Ps. 83:11 (RSV = Ps. 84:10).

who must keep her children always tied to her apron strings instead of sending them away to live their own lives and fulfill their own destinies, is the "devouring mother" of the psychologists; and in destroying her children's vocations, she also inevitably destroys her own. The pompous father with the lust for power, who is always laying down the law and refusing to listen to any point of view but his own, is again turning power into tyranny.

You may find parents wrecking their children's lives by preventing them from making the marriage of their choice for snobbish or other illegitimate reasons.

You may find parents (of the kind who would be regarded as devout Catholics) being horrified at the thought of their daughter entering a convent, and doing everything in their power to stop her. On the other hand, there are the parents whose great ambition is to see their son a priest and who will work relentlessly, and in defiance of his own real aptitudes and desires, to indoctrinate him with the idea that it is his ambition too — so that perhaps he finds only when it is too late that it was not his vocation at all.

Then there are the mothers who keep a rigid control over their children's lives and activities by the simple expedient of becoming gravely ill whenever there is the least sign of insurrection. And there are the mothers with iron constitutions who are nevertheless so frail and ailing that their daughters have to give up all thought of marriage or career in order to be always by them, to be their nursemaids and domestic drudges.

There are husbands who want to use their wives simply as social assets, and will in consequence force them into a mold which is completely uncongenial to them. There are others who will demand their marital rights in the name of good, solid Catholic doctrine, with complete disregard for the desires and sometimes even the health of their partners.

On the other hand, there are wives of the dominating, matriarchal type, who will spend their time and their inexhaustible energies running Catholic clubs and guilds and committees and becoming a power in the parish, blissfully unaware that they are driving their unfortunate husbands to drink or some other form of escape from an intolerable situation. There are others who have learned the commercial value of tears, and who will open the floodgates with complete lack of conscience at the first hint of opposition to their selfish and irresponsible whims.

Children, in their turn, can be shrewd in discovering just the right technique for making their parents do what they want, and ruthless in exploiting it.

And in all these relationships *l'appétit grandit en mangeant*: to have once tasted the delights of power and exploitation will almost certainly mean to want more and more of them; and so it is that many a marriage and many a home are wrecked. And it is always essentially the same thing: whenever husbands and wives or parents and children treat each other simply as means to a selfish gratification — whether, in fact, they spoil them or are harsh to them, whether they fetter them or exploit them, whether they treat them as playthings or turn them into drudges — it always means the abuse of a God-given authority or power for purely selfish purposes.

As in the home, so in the civic community, or for that matter, in religious communities, men can be led to seek for power and office in order to minister to their own pride and selfishness and self-esteem. And the same is true, not merely of power and position, but of possessions of every kind. We are absolute owners of nothing; we are only stewards; but we are very quick to forget that fact. When we "count our blessings," we do not always recall that they are, in fact, blessings: gifts from God which we have done nothing to deserve, and which are given to us for His purposes and not ours. Only the poor in spirit — who are never selfish about their possessions, never miserly, but, on the contrary, are prodigal with all they have, all their material possessions and all their gifts of body and mind and soul — are Christlike in their use of power or property. And we know all too well by bitter experience how difficult it is for us with our vaulting ambitions or petty greeds to achieve poverty of spirit.

But we have to remember, too, how easy it is for us to deceive ourselves, to rationalize, and to find respectable or even noble reasons for making what is, in fact, a purely selfish use of the good things God has given us. We delude ourselves into thinking that ambition or the lust for power are really zeal for God's house or enthusiasm for an ideal or a loving concern to better the lot of our fellowmen. We see in our greed only a natural and even laudable desire for life's necessities.

The bread in this story can stand as a symbol of all the good things of life which we naturally and inevitably desire: affection, security, comfort, joy, pleasure, rest, relief from pain or strain or worry, and the enjoyment of health and well-being. We cannot help craving for them; but we can, and ought to, avoid feeling sorry for ourselves if we fail to find them. From self-pity it is a very short step to grumbling and blaming God, and to the sort of arrogance which demands these things as a right and, if they are withheld, will see in some form of self-indulgence only a legitimate compensation. And when we do that, we are doing what Satan does: we are not turning stones into bread, but bread into stones, perverting the good things of life by putting them to evil uses.

We do well to beware of the Devil's bread. "What man is there among you," our Lord asked, "of whom if his son shall ask bread, will he reach him a stone?" And He goes on: "If you, then, being evil, know how to give good gifts to your children, how much more will your Father who is in Heaven give good things to them that ask Him?"[170] Good things: these things that come to us from God may not, at first sight, seem good; they may indeed be hard and costing; but faith will look beyond the immediate hardship to an ultimate benefit, beyond the immediate sorrow to an ultimate joy. So it is that God, in the end, always turns stones into bread.

With Satan it is the other way round. The gifts he offers are, at first sight, brave and glittering things, and so we clutch at them as though they were necessities we could not possibly do without; but disillusionment swiftly follows, and what we thought to be bread proves to be only a stone. So the rich man in the parable, when his lands brought forth abundant crops, forgot all about God and set himself to build bigger barns, to take his ease, and to eat, drink, and be merry; and all to no purpose, for immediately his soul was required of him.[171]

The Devil's bread leads only to emptiness and disillusionment. God's bread brings strength and fulfillment. There is a

[170] Matt. 7:9, 11.
[171] Luke 12:16-21.

prefiguring of it in the story of Elijah, who was miraculously fed and who walked for forty days in the strength that the bread gave him until he came to the mountain of God.[172] The divine Bread does not shield us from hardship — there is still the forty days' journey to be done — but it gives us the strength and courage to meet the hardship, and it brings us to God's home in the end.

"But," Jesus answered the Devil, "it is written, 'Not by bread alone doth man live, but by every word that proceedeth from the mouth of God.' "[173] Why was our Lord at pains to make any reply? Why did He not merely silence the Devil, or rebuke him as later He rebuked Peter: "Get thee behind me, Satan"?[174]

Presumably because He wished to show us how to deal with temptation in our turn. First, His ordeal was preceded by His baptism: our first line of defense against evil is to make the best use we can of the sacraments. Then He sought the solitude of the desert: and we, too, need to be often alone with God if we are to acquire the wisdom and the strength we need. Next, His prayer and fasting: these, too, are basic needs for us; He was Himself to say later on that there are some spirits which yield only to prayer and fasting, to a deep communion with God and a spirit of self-denial. And now, in His answer to Satan, He gives us the final lesson. "All Scripture is inspired by God and useful for teaching, for correcting, for instructing in justice, so that the man of God may be perfect,

---

[172] 3 Kings 19:8 (RSV = 1 Kings 19:8).
[173] Matt. 4:4; Deut. 8:3.
[174] Matt. 16:23; Mark 8:33.

equipped for every good work":[175] equipped, too, to meet tempt
tation successfully.

But merely to be learned in the Scriptures is not enough:
the Devil himself is that. It is not enough just to say that man
does not live by bread alone: we need the strong faith that will
convince us, in mind and in heart, that the saying is true.
Without faith the Scriptures are an unlighted torch. Our
Lord's text, showing us the supreme value of God's word, shows
us at the same time the importance of its correlative, a loving
faith in that word. How indeed can we hope to resist the
blandishments of evil unless we are strongly drawn to the
good, to God and His word and His will? It is for this that we
need the sacraments, the solitude, the prayer, and the self-
control: to see and understand and love the will of God, and
to have hope, as well as faith and charity. Recurrent temptation may make us depressed and discouraged, perhaps even to
the point of giving up the struggle; hope will give us the
strength to continue, putting our trust not in our own efforts
but in God, and refusing to take our constant failures as final.
We may think we see no sign of progress in spite of all our
labors: we forget that continuing to struggle is itself a sign of
progress.

When our Lord desired that Peter should be strengthened
so as to be able, in turn, to strengthen his brethren, He prayed
that his *faith* would not fail.[176] Faith is the fundamental thing
in the Christian life: everything else must be built on that. If
you want to progress in the moral virtues, you are wise to see

[175] 2 Tim. 3:16-17.
[176] Luke 22:32.

an increase of faith as the first step: let your faith become deeper, more vivid, and more compelling, and the rest will follow. And in your own efforts to live a better life, the emphasis will be where it ought to be: on God. Some traditions of spirituality do, in fact, put the emphasis on the moral virtues, on human striving for perfection, on rigid techniques of self-analysis and self-examination, on ascetical practices, on the discovery and uprooting of all imperfections, and on meditations dealing with moral topics. The danger there lies in the egocentric character of the emphasis, the turning inward of the soul's attention upon itself.

Oculi mei semper ad Dominum: My eyes are ever toward the Lord.[177] If, while trying as hard as you can to lead a moral life, you always think of any success, not as something you achieve for yourself, but as something God achieves in you — if, in other words, you look always to God in faith and hope — then your life acquires a theocentric emphasis, and moral endeavor is firmly set in its proper context as part of your faith in God and your worship and love of Him. Your life, moreover, will acquire a breadth, a serenity, a childlike quality, which it might otherwise lack. Failure can quickly undermine self-confidence; it will not quickly undermine a Christ-confidence which is the fruit of faith, hope, and love.

A too-meticulous concern for the minutiae of morality and for one's own efforts in dealing with them can cause one to lose sight of the grand basic realities, of God and His love and His care; it can also very easily induce a timid or fretful anxiety which is far from being in keeping with the "liberty of the sons

---

[177] Ps. 24:15 (RSV = Ps. 25:15).

of God."[178] And, finally, it can be very remote from that childlike attitude toward God which our Lord bids us adopt. The child is normally without anxiety about things which worry his parents: he has confidence that they will see that he is fed and clothed, will guard him from danger, and will comfort him if he is hurt. He is not concerned over his lack of earning power or his small size or feeble strength. He feels that the situation is in good hands; his parents will be equal to any crisis or emergency that may arise; it is not on his own strength or power that he depends but on his parents', and therefore he can be serene and content. He cannot, of course, leave everything to his parents: he has to make his own efforts and learn to do things for himself; but in making those efforts, he feels behind him his parents' sustaining hands, and his faith in them gives him faith in himself.

"Man does not live by bread alone." As we have seen, our Lord was here quoting from Deuteronomy, and we may presume that He would quote the Hebrew text, although the quotation as we have it in the Gospel is from the Septuagint, a free translation intended to clarify the Hebrew idiom for Greek readers. Moses was telling his hearers that when bread failed them in the desert, God would not abandon them, but would devise other means of feeding them; and this he expressed by saying that man lives not by bread alone but by "everything that comes forth from the mouth of God," i.e., by whatever God shall ordain for the purpose.

Here too, then, we can take the text in its literal meaning as a firm expression of trust in God's Providence: if He deprives

---

[178] Rom. 8:21.

us of bread, He will see to it that we are fed in some other way. But even when bread is available, it is not of itself enough to satisfy man's needs: there must also be the command of God. If He were, in fact, to turn the stones into bread, what would it profit Him unless it were God's will that He should do so? Satan argues that bread is a necessity; our Lord must have it, and He has the power to procure it: it would be wrong for Him therefore not to do so. Our Lord does not deny that under ordinary circumstances bread is a necessity; but He does deny that it is an ultimate or absolute necessity. "Even though He slay me, yet will I trust Him":[179] if God were to deny us food for the body, it would be to show us, to give us, something even more essential.

What applies to bread can be applied also to all the things we need or think we need or find desirable: Satan will try to persuade us that they are absolute necessities, so that if they are refused us, we see ourselves as the victims of divine injustice; he will also try to make us think that in the achieving of perhaps perfectly good ends, our own efforts — the means we would like to adopt because they are congenial — are both necessary and sufficient. In fact, even the most perfect means will profit us nothing unless God blesses them, unless they are the means which He chooses for us. "Unless the Lord build the house, they labor in vain that build it. Unless the Lord keep the city, he watcheth in vain that keepeth it."[180] That is the point of saying grace at meals, and of blessing not only food and drink, but all the other things we use in our daily lives. It

[179] Cf. Job 13:15.
[180] Ps. 126:1 (RSV = Ps. 127:1).

is the point, too, of spiritual healing, that "laying on of hands" to restore the sick which figured so prominently in the early Church,[181] but which now, unfortunately, apart from the sacrament of the Anointing of the Sick, has ceased to loom large in our lives.

All of God's creatures, great and little, look to God, as the psalmist tells us, "to send them their food at the appointed time; it is through Thy gift that they find it; Thy hand opens and all are filled with content";[182] or, as the monastic grace before meals puts it, "Thou fillest every living creature with Thy *blessing*." It is not the bread of our choosing that brings us life: not the things we decide to be good or necessary for us; not the joys we yearn for and the pleasures after which we hanker; not the health, the prosperity, the friends, the popularity, the successful careers, and the rewarding achievements. Not these things in themselves, but only these things if willed by God, and therefore blessed by God, will truly bring us life.

So the psalmist tells us again: "From Thy high dwelling place, Thou dost send rain upon the hills; Thy hand gives the earth all her plenty." And therefore, because of that beneficent hand, the grass will grow for the cattle, and for man the earth will put forth her shoots that there may be bread and oil and wine to strengthen him and gladden his heart. "Thou dost decree darkness, and night falls; in the night, all the forest is astir with prowling beasts; the young lions go roaring after their prey, God's pensioners, asking for their food." First the will, the blessing; only then the food. For "if Thou turnest

---

[181] Cf. Acts 28:8.
[182] Ps. 103:27-28 (Knox; RSV = Ps. 104:27-28).

away Thy face, they shall be troubled: Thou shalt take away their breath, and they shall fail, and shall go back to the dust they came from."[183]

At the same time, given God's blessing, it is possible for man to live even though he may have very little bread, very meager material resources. A little oil and wheat sufficed to feed Elijah and the poor widow and her son for a long time;[184] and five loaves and two fishes were more than enough for the feeding of the five thousand.[185] True, we cannot normally expect miracles; but normally our temptation is the opposite one of wanting the sense of security given by abundant resources. We find it very hard to be poor in spirit, and therefore we find it very hard to have that carefree trust in God which is characteristic of the saints. They, for their part, are suspicious of material riches and endowments as a foundation for their work for God. So Dominic,[186] when he began his apostolate among the Albigenses, dispensed with the rich panoply and trappings of his predecessors in the field and went poor and on foot. So Francis,[187] before wedding Lady Poverty, dispensed even with his clothes and left them behind him in the piazza. The Church has often enough been ill-served by good but unimaginative men who resorted to "rich means" to advance Her cause; and the amassing of wealth in a good cause

[183] Ps. 103:13-15, 20-21, 29 (RSV = Ps. 104:13-15, 20-21, 29).
[184] 3 Kings 17:10-15 (RSV = 1 Kings 17:10-15).
[185] Matt. 14:19-21; Mark 6:41-42; Luke 9:16-17.
[186] St. Dominic (1170-1221), the founder of the Order of Friars Preachers.
[187] St. Francis of Assisi (1182-1226), founder of the Franciscan Order.

can very easily degenerate into the hoarding or spending of it in a bad one.

In fact, it is possible to go hungry in the midst of plenty, like the millionaire whose ravaged health forces him to live on barley water and dry biscuits. All the wealth in the world will not give us the good things of life if God does not will us to enjoy them, if injury or disease or circumstance keeps us from them. In spite of their quail and their manna, many of the Israelites perished; while on the other hand, Daniel and his companions flourished on the coarse meats with which they were fed and, indeed, looked stronger and fairer than all the children who were given the king's own food to eat.[188]

Perhaps it is to underline the merely relative importance of material means, and of human endowments generally, that God sometimes dispenses with them altogether. In the desert, there was literally no bread and He sent the manna, just as at Cana, there was literally no more wine and He gave them wine with what had been water.[189] Again, He often uses the most unlikely material as means to His ends, as when He used clay and spittle to give sight to the blind man.[190] Order and beauty are brought forth from chaos: the light shines forth out of darkness; water flows from the dry rock; the divine genealogy is studded with the names of harlots and sinners; the cowardly and impulsive Peter becomes the steady rock on which the Church is built; and the human source of that living mind of the Church, which we call Christian tradition, was the little

[188] Dan. 1:15.
[189] John 2:3-10.
[190] John 9:6-7.

group of ignorant fishermen who became the Apostolic College. Again and again God uses the weak and foolish to confound the wise;[191] it is the harlots and sinners, He tells us, who enter the kingdom of Heaven first;[192] it is from the mouths of the babes and sucklings that He looks for perfect praise.[193]

Humility is truth, accepting the real facts about ourselves, and sometimes we sin against it by overconfidence, by exaggerating our gifts and putting all our trust in a strength which is largely illusory; but sometimes we sin in the opposite sense, by minimizing our gifts, by pretending we are less or worse than we really are. Truth lies in accepting ourselves while realizing both that whatever good there is in us comes from God and that, however insignificant our endowments are, God is quite capable of achieving through us the ends He desires if only we will accept His will and trust in Him. She who sang of her own lowliness sang also of the great things that He who is mighty had done in her; and to Him, in consequence, she gave praise.[194] Even in her Son, there is that same unexpectedness: "Can anything good come out of Nazareth?" they cried, little knowing that what had, in fact, come was the Light of the World.[195]

All of these thoughts are suggested by our Lord's quotation in its original text and context. But, as Lagrange points out, He who came to bring the Law its plenitude was under no

[191] Cf. 1 Cor. 1:27.
[192] Matt. 21:31.
[193] Matt. 21:16; Ps. 8:3 (RSV = Ps. 8:2).
[194] Luke 1:49.
[195] John 1:46, 8:12, 9:5.

obligation to adhere to the strict literal sense of the Hebrew; and we can find further food for thought if we turn to the Septuagint.

Man lives not by bread alone but by "every word that proceedeth from the mouth of God." Here we can take *word*, not as meaning the providing by God of some substitute nourishment (such as the manna in the desert), but as being itself nourishment, the nourishment not of the body but of the soul. In other words, we have a life more important than the life of the body, and the food which nourishes this other life, the life of the spirit, is the word of God, the expressed will of God.

All Catholics would, of course, agree that the supernatural life is more important than the natural and that the Church's primary concern is with the former and not the latter. But it is possible to be muddled in one's thinking about some of the applications of these general truths, especially in the context of social justice and social reform. The Church is often accused of being indifferent to poverty, squalor, illiteracy, and social evils of one sort or another; and although the accusations come normally from outside, they are sometimes reflected in an attitude of mind among Catholics themselves. Various influences come together to make up this attitude of mind. There are the accusations themselves, whether true or false; there is the influence on our thinking of Marxism at one extreme and of the papal encyclicals on social justice at the other; there is, in some cases, a sort of guilt-feeling, perhaps not wholly conscious, about the callousness and, indeed, cruelty which loom so large in some of the chapters of our Catholic history; and there is the fact that we live in an age of social consciousness, of such experiments as the welfare state, and of the wonderful work done by priests and other Catholics in the cause of social justice.

Now, this mixture of good things and bad, of truths and half-truths and falsehoods, can make for a muddled outlook. The two extremes are clear: on the one hand, the old adage "Don't preach to a starving man; give him bread" remains as true as ever; on the other, it is wrong to heap material gifts on one's relatives, dependents, friends, and the world at large, while damaging or destroying their souls. But between these extremes, there is an area in which it is easy to get things wrong, to see the work of the Church in the world too exclusively in terms of social activity.

We may learn a lesson here from the story of Judas and Mary Magdalene. We are told that Mary brought a pot of precious spikenard and anointed the feet of Jesus, and that thereupon Judas angrily complained, "Wherefore this waste? This might have been sold for much and given to the poor."[196] There is a curiously modern ring to this complaint; and at first sight, it is certainly very plausible. Many similar things have been said in recent times by social demagogues and reformers, indignant at aristocratic privilege or the furs and jewels of the rich. How can that woman wear mink while many people shiver with the cold? How can those people dine at the Ritz while multitudes cry out for bread?

But Judas's argument, in fact, rests on a number of fallacies. In the first place, on the purely economic level, if you took all the wealth of all the millionaires in the world and distributed it to the poor, it would work out at some quite small sum

[196] John 12:3-5.

apiece, so that it would seem hardly worth all the trouble; and the logical conclusion of that sort of train of thought is that no one is entitled to spend on himself any money above the level of the most indigent human being alive, a conclusion which few would regard as either acceptable or practical. But in the second place, to take the thing on the purely economic level is itself the essential fallacy: Mary's action is a lovely gesture of love and gratitude, of far more value to mankind than a free meal.

Even naturally speaking, without any thought of super-natural values, bread is not the most important thing in life, once we exist above starvation or penury level. True, we live in a world which extols the supremacy of material and utili-tarian things, a world in which the poets and artists who are prepared to starve rather than stop being poets and artists are regarded as fools. In education, in life in general, the humani-ties are more and more disregarded in favor of commercially rewarding subjects and pursuits.

We forget that, in Browning's phrase, the sauce to meat is ceremony; we forget the importance of pageantry; we forget that unless there is grace in living, life is hardly worth living at all, and without poetry the world is a prosaic world, a drab world. And because we forget these things, we are in danger of becoming the most impoverished of all human civilizations. Yet, as individuals, we all know the thrilling effect on us of a magnificent gesture, an unforgettable moment of revelation in art, in music, in drama, or in love; we know that these are the all-too-rare moments which lift us right out of the normal prosaic routine and renew our hearts: and are we to call these waste?

The Devil

St. Augustine remarks that Mary Magdalene was the only sinner who sought out our Lord not for any bodily relief or comfort, but simply to beg forgiveness of her sins. And having received that forgiveness, she could not do enough to express her gratitude and her love: she brought her precious ointment, but she had to use it all, she had to pour it all out — and have we not all known, loved, and treasured similar prodigalities of love? — so that, we are told, the whole house was filled with the scent of it, and our Lord foretold that it would fill the whole world. There is an obvious parallel here with the mighty wind which filled the whole house on the first Pentecost,[197] and which thereafter also filled the whole world — "*Spiritus Domini replevit totam orbem terrarum,*" as we say in the Mass for Pentecost — for indeed spikenard and wind are both Love.

Judas is plausible, for it is true that waste is wrong, and caring for the poor is good, and zeal in their cause is good. But we are told his hidden, perhaps not wholly conscious, motive: he was a thief; and so, from talking now of selling the ointment, he will come in the end to selling Christ.[198]

Our Lord denies that it is waste; He declares it a good deed; He says that wherever the Gospel is preached, Mary's act will be remembered.[199] And why this unique commendation, if not to give a dramatic rebuke to our materialism, our money-grubbing, and our utilitarianism? When Mary gives the whole of the ointment to God, she is giving her whole self to God in

[197] Acts 2:2.
[198] John 12:6; Matt. 26:15.
[199] Matt. 26:13.

joyful prodigality; and there is nothing in the world more important than that.

When our Lord preached in the synagogue at the beginning of His ministry, He read the passage in which Isaiah describes how the Spirit sent Him out "to preach the gospel to the poor, to restore the broken-hearted; to bid the prisoners go free, and the blind receive their sight."[200] That is the true order of things. Communists and others who have no belief in Providence or in eternal life must of necessity think only in terms of bread, of natural needs, and look only to their own efforts or the efforts of the state for the establishment of social justice. That is essentially just what Satan wanted to induce Christ to do; and Christ rebuked him by putting things in their true order: first we must serve God, and only then must we be concerned with bread; and our efforts to earn our bread can never be dissociated from our worship of God — they must always be within the framework of God's will and His care for us.

The same is true of the Church: Her first concern must always be the worship of God; Her second concern, bringing souls to God, to eternal life; and only in the third place can She be concerned for men's temporal welfare. Even in times of crisis, such as famines and plagues, the Church must be less concerned with remedying the crises than with seeing that the dying receive the sacraments. A Vincent de Paul[201] is deeply concerned with the temporal needs of the poor, yes; but his

---

[200] Luke 4:18-19 (Knox); Isa. 61:1.

[201] St. Vincent de Paul (c. 1580-1660), founder of the Lazarist Fathers and the Sisters of Charity.

primary concern, like Christ's, is to preach the gospel to them, to save their souls.

Those who taunt the Church with fobbing off the poor with promises of pie in the sky instead of feeding them here and now are exactly reproducing Satan's argument; and those Catholics who see the Church's work primarily in terms of social work are, in effect, thinking along the same lines. Between the two extremes of giving absolute primacy to bread, on the one hand, and being quite indifferent to a lack of bread, to accumulating social evils, on the other, there is the true order of things: to pray and labor for the temporal welfare of the poor and needy, but still more to pray and labor for their eternal welfare.

To *pray:* it is not only, or perhaps even primarily, the social workers who help the poor: it is the contemplatives. *Aperis tu manum tuam:* to believe in Providence and prayer at all is to believe that in answer to prayer, God will "open His hand and fill every creature with His blessing." Just as an individual's work for the poor will not be likely to prosper unless he calls down God's blessing upon it by prayer, so with the work of the Church as a whole: there are some whose destiny takes them among the poor, the sick, and the destitute, and they try to save these souls by ministering to their temporal needs; but behind their efforts is the power of their own prayer, and behind that is the prayer of all those whose lives are given to prayer, and the prayer of the whole Church.

We may well lament the fact that *Rerum Novarum* was not better heeded when first it was given to the world; we may well regret that other similar directives at other times have fallen on deaf ears; and we cannot prize or praise too highly the work that is being done in the Church for social justice today; but it remains true that the primary work of the Church is spiritual, attending to the supernatural needs of the faithful.

And even here we have an important lesson to learn from Mary Magdalene, for here, too, bread — supernatural bread — is not enough. Certainly it is bread we have to pray for first of all, the grace to obey the ordinary basic rules of the Christian life, the Ten Commandments. That is much more than most of us can ever hope to manage; but it is not enough. That is the prose of the Christian life; and however immature and unsuccessful we may be, we need the poetry. The Christian life is too often painted for us by moralists and preachers who are purely prosaic, and perhaps even prosy, and that is a great tragedy because it is a distortion. Present it in terms merely of character-training, of acquiring the moral virtues, and you dechristianize it, for there is nothing specifically Christian about being prudent and just and brave and self-controlled.

The Christian ideal at which we have to aim, however remotely, is not just virtuous conduct but holiness, and *holiness* means being possessed by the Spirit: the Wind that bloweth where it listeth, and no man knoweth whence it cometh nor whither it goeth.[202] That is the poetry of the Christian life, and that is the reason why the saints are so exciting, so spontaneous, so unpredictable: for they are what we all ought to be, the troubadours of God.

That is the ultimate lesson to be learned from Mary Magdalene. There is loveliness in the prodigality of lovers, and without it, the world would be a mean and penurious place;

[202] John 3:8.

but the greatest loveliness of all is the prodigality of the saints, who pour out all they have in total self-offering to God and to the world. They, above all, are the ones who know that bread is of little importance beside the word of God and who give their lives totally and triumphantly to fulfilling that word.

Is God's word always fulfilled? In one sense, absolutely speaking, yes. *Omnia quaecumque voluit fecit:* "Our God is a God that dwells in Heaven; all that His will designs, He executes."[203] For "this is the God who makes His word known to Jacob, gives Israel ruling and decree"; "see how He issues His commands to the earth, how swiftly His word runs! Now He spreads a pall of snow . . . binds the waters at the onset of His frost. Then, at His word, all melts away; a breath from Him, and the waters flow!"[204] This is the word in which all things have their beginning, their evolution, their being; it is the Word through whom all things were made; it embraces all things which God commands or at least permits to be, which is to say, quite simply, all things, for nothing could exist unless God at least allowed it to be. This, then, is the word which created the universe and the physical laws which govern it, and which bestows on us all the things we count as blessings, the good things of life both natural and supernatural.

But there is a sense in which we can speak of God's word, or will, as not being always fulfilled: the word which God would have fulfilled had He not, for the sake of some greater good, allowed it to remain undone. Under this heading come, not the physical laws which govern the conduct of the universe,

[203] Ps. 113:11 (Knox; RSV = Ps. 115:3).
[204] Ps. 147:9, 4-8 (Knox; RSV = Ps. 147:19, 15-18).

but the moral laws which ought to govern the conduct of man. We have the terrifying power of opposing and, in a sense, nullifying God's will, even though, in the last resort, it is His will to allow us to do so.

That is why in all sin there is an appalling pride, because all sin is an arrogation to ourselves of the sovereignty of God. Not Thy will, but mine be done.[205] And when we try to be as gods we die the death: the tree of life becomes for us the tree of death. But to try to live by the word of God is to find the opposite: the tree of death becomes the tree of life, and the arid rock becomes a fountain of water springing up into life everlasting.

The Word tells us that we must not be solicitous about what we shall eat or drink or wherewith we shall be clothed: we must seek first the kingdom of God and all these things shall be added to us.[206] He is not, of course, telling us that we must have no care or concern for our needs, our well-being, no thought for the future; He is not abrogating the earlier decree that we must earn our bread by the sweat of our brow.[207] He is telling us not to be *solicitous*: not to be anxious with the anxiety of the man who feels he has no one to rely on but himself. He is telling us to trust our heavenly Father: to be ready, if need be, to forgo things that seem desirable or even necessary rather than do anything contrary to God's will, confident that if we do so, we shall not be losers in the end. It is worthwhile, He tells us, to go hungry or cold or naked now

---

[205] Cf. Luke 22:42.
[206] Matt. 6:31, 33.
[207] Gen. 3:19.

if it means, in the end, being filled with the infinity of God. No command of His will harm us in the end, however strange or even terrible it may at first appear.

It is significant that the words *Deus providebit,* "God will provide," the motto so often used to express trust in God's care and loving kindness, were spoken by Abraham when he had been commanded by God to take his son, his only-begotten Isaac, whom he loved, and offer him in sacrifice. There is a strange and often terrible irony to be found in the history of God's dealings with men. Abraham was to take the boy "into the land of vision";[208] and the boy's name means "laughter";[209] but what God was asking was that Abraham should see the end of all laughter, the destruction of all his hopes, and the abolition of all God's promises to him. And it was when, on the way, the boy asked him, "Here are wood and fire, but where is the victim?" that his father sadly parried the question by telling him, "God will provide."[210]

Many commentators are at great pains to exonerate God from the shame of demanding something so deeply offensive to their sense of justice and humanity. Some go into long disquisitions on the way in which the prevalence of human sacrifice among the Canaanites would have affected Abraham's moral standards, as though that were any help; others give great emphasis to the fact that God did not really want the sacrifice to be carried out, forgetting that if a thing is wrong to do, it is wrong to command. They forget that God

[208] Gen. 22:2.
[209] Gen. 21:6.
[210] Gen. 22:7-8.

decreed an even more terrible sacrifice of an only Son, a sacrifice which was indeed carried out, and in which it was not Abraham's heart that was broken.

The problem is, in fact, a pseudo-problem because it is based on a confusion. God could not possibly command a man to lie, to steal, or to murder; but a lie is always a lie, whereas the taking of life is not always a murder. God is the Lord of life; it is His to give and to take away, whether directly or indirectly. No doubt we would be less humanitarian about physical death if we were more hopeful about the afterlife, and less concerned about the land of the living if we were more concerned with the land of vision. God did not, in fact, desire human sacrifice, and He took this dramatic way of teaching His people so.

But the important point for us is that there are few things harder to say than: "Even though He slay me, yet will I trust Him," and that one of them is: "Even though He cause me to slay my only son, my Laughter, yet will I trust Him"; and it is because of that gigantic act of faith and trust and obedience that we recall the sacrifice of Abraham every day in the Mass.[211]

But in Abraham's story, the life and the laughter were given back to him; and in the story of humanity as a whole, the same is true. The last word is *laughter:* not the heartfree "sunburnt mirth"[212] of the merry, feckless pagan, but the heartfelt Son-given laughter of the sons of God, who have known sorrow but have seen it turned into joy. They are the ones who, when

---

[211] Eucharistic Prayer I.

[212] John Keats, "Ode to a Nightingale," stanza 2.

things go wrong, will not despair or grumble; who really do seek first the kingdom of Heaven; who can laugh at their pains because already they have learned how to laugh for joy. They know deep in their hearts that in the end "the blessing of the Lord maketh men rich; neither shall affliction be joined to them,"[213] and they wait in faith, hope, and patient expectancy for the day when laughter shall no more be the fugitive and fragmentary thing it is for most of us on earth, but the abiding laughter which is the sound of the Light Inaccessible,[214] the ripples on the surface of the eternal sea of peace and joy.

[213] Prov. 10:22.
[214] 1 Tim. 6:16.

Chapter Five

The Perils of the Pinnacle

"Then the Devil took Him up into the holy city, and set Him upon the pinnacle of the temple."[215]

Satan is a subtle opportunist and knows how to draw victory out of defeat. A man may avoid one pitfall only to find that, in the subsequent glow of self-gratulation and overconfidence, he at once falls into another, perhaps a worse one. So, in Satan's attack upon our Lord, in the first assault he is defeated, but out of his defeat he draws material for a fresh attempt. He had tried to induce Christ, in His hunger and want, to distrust the power and gentleness of God, but Christ had replied by a strong affirmation of His trust. Now, therefore, he will try the opposite tactic: try to induce in Him an excess of trust, in the sense of a wanton presumption: "If You are the Son of God, cast Yourself down, for God will then send angels to save You from being dashed against the rocks below."[216] The

---

[215] Matt. 4:5.
[216] Cf. Matt. 4:6.

implication is not merely that God will, in fact, send angels, but that He must: it is an arrogant attempt to force God's hand. It is one thing to trust in God even in the worst extremities; it is quite another to presume on His goodness to minister to our vanity.

Satan is subtle, too, in his choice of a setting. The desert was the appropriate place for the first temptation: in an arid, unpeopled wilderness, it is easy to fall into melancholy, to feel a desolation and affliction of spirit, to feel the lack of human companionship, human sympathy, or perhaps admiration. And in such conditions, it is easy to fall a victim to sensual temptations of some kind, for nature then inclines us to look for pleasures by way of compensation for the feelings of sadness and desolation.

But for a temptation to presumption, the pinnacle of the temple was an excellent choice. Elevation lends itself to presumption: there is a giddiness of mind that can easily result from being lifted high above others and looking down on them. And this high place was in the city: no solitude now, but the bustle of social and civic life, the bustle of ambition in particular.

"These little figures running about like ants far below are all relentlessly driven by dreams of success; some want to be rich, some to be popular and applauded; some want power, prestige, and social standing. And their cult of success will force them to salute success. You want to win their allegiance; it is Your duty to do so; You must, then, accommodate Yourself to their ways of thought. However, stand out against them, be poor and humble, be a failure, and You will lose them. And what pride, to claim to be so different from them!

The Perils of the Pinnacle

"This is not just any city: it is the holy city, and you are looking down on holy places, the courts of the temple, and on holy men, the priests of the temple. At least you cannot claim to be so different from these. Perhaps you will see Ananias:[217] look into his heart, and you will see that he is so blinded, he would be ready to decry God's ultimate truth as a blasphemy. Look at Caiaphas:[218] he is a man who would sacrifice a sacred principle, a man's life, and his own soul, for the sake of expediency. Look at those Pharisees, with their long prayers and their long faces, their proud assumption of superiority because of a holiness which is, in fact, merely an empty insistence on legal minutiae. But these are chosen souls, specially dedicated to God's service and held in deep respect by their fellowmen: who are You to condemn them?"

We are gregarious animals. We like to fit in with the crowd. Unless we are very staunch individualists, we may easily follow a natural inclination, a sort of psychological herd-instinct, and adopt, perhaps quite unconsciously, the ways of thought and the moral standards which are admired and approved by those among whom we live. Fervor can easily turn into laxity by force of environment, and the integrity of faith can become lost in a fog of compromise. We live in a climate of opinion which tends to take Christian standards of life as, at best, an impractical idealism, and Christian dogma as an outmoded fantasy. Nothing is easier than to sink imperceptibly into an attitude of mind which will concede that perhaps we Christians do set our sights too high, that perhaps our standards are

[217] Cf. Acts 23:1-2.
[218] John 11:49-50.

a little exaggerated for the workaday world, and that we are being rather foolish in attaching importance to things which the world regards as of no moment at all.

But it is not only the non-Christian world which can thus cause us to abandon our intellectual integrity. The city of Christ's temptation was the holy city, the city of priests and Scribes and Pharisees. The Catholic girl leaves her convent school and begins to take an adult part in contemporary Catholic life; the convert, fresh from his or her blinding discovery of God, of Christ, and of the divine thing we call the Church, enters into the ordinary activities included under the heading of "modern Catholicism": what do they find? They find indeed the same essential divinity, in the Mass, in the sacraments, in prayer, in great and humble souls, and in the innumerable kindnesses and generosities which express, in ordinary human circumstances, the majesty of the charity of Christ. But they may meet also — and with who can tell what shock of disillusionment and dismay — another side of the picture. They may meet the modern high priest and the modern Pharisee; they may discover just how sordid the motivations of pious people can be; they may meet the black-hearted dévotes of Mauriac's[219] novels, or the smart Catholics and the snob Catholics; they may see, as Christ saw, the house of God turned into a den of thieves.[220] Above all, they may meet the sanctimonious assumption that if, in defiance of Browning, all is wrong with the world,[221] still all is right with the Church:

[219] François Mauriac (1885-1970), French author.

[220] Matt. 21:13.

[221] Cf. "All's right with the world"; Robert Browning, "Pippa Passes," Part 1.

they may discover that if the occupational disease of modern communism is brainwashing, the occupational disease of some modern Catholics is whitewashing.

And if they are great souls, all this will sadden them; but if they are little souls — and the Church exists primarily for God's little ones — these scandals may make them cynical. If this sort of thing is to be found among the great ones whom Catholics revere and adulate, what hope is there of finding any integrity in anyone? Cynicism, it is true, is often a rather pitiable defense mechanism: if you disbelieve in ideals, you are saved from the self-reproach of not pursuing them; if you disbelieve in motives in general, it absolves you from the necessity of inquiring too closely into your own. But what a terrible tragedy it is if the cynicism and delinquency of the juvenile, disillusioned about his parents and starved of love in his home, is paralleled by the cynicism and delinquency of the young or new Catholic, disillusioned about life in the Church and starved of love in the home of Christ!

There is danger in being set upon a pinnacle because of what you can see from that eminence; there is still more danger in the fact that you can *be* seen from there. St. Augustine speaks in his Rule of those who, being in positions of greater authority, are therefore in greater danger. It is a terrible thing to be responsible to God for another human being, as husbands and wives are responsible for each other, as parents are responsible for their children, and as friend is responsible for friend. How much more terrible when the responsibility is not an individual but a general one!

In the Church, some have greatness thrust upon them; and if they should fail in any way, we can only have sympathy for them and pray for them; if we sink so low as to condemn any man for weakness, we shall be in the company of those for whose benefit Christ stooped down and wrote in the sand.[222] But some thrust themselves into prominence, whether as "leading laymen" or as "eminent ecclesiastics"; and then you may well see the scandal of power and influence being put to shoddy or arrogant or even satanic purposes. To be perched on a pinnacle may be soothing to our vanity; but how much safer to be sitting quietly at the back of the church with the poor and the humble who are never in the public eye, but only in the eye and heart of God.

St. Paul speaks of preaching to others and becoming himself a castaway: it is a possibility that can never be far from the mind of any who have to exert power or influence over others, unless they are entrenched in self-righteousness. True, it is no solution to stop preaching until one is worthy to preach; if that were done, the pulpits, let us hope, would all be empty. All we can do in such a situation is to go on as best we can with the work given to us to do, and to try to avoid distressing others by any flaunting of our sins. The fact remains that words exercise much less influence than deeds, although both are necessary. One saint does infinitely more good in the world than a hundred eloquent preachers. It is easy to hear the truth and do nothing about it; it is harder not to be fired by a real enthusiasm, by the lovely contagion of real holiness: *Si vis me flere, dolendum est primum ipsi tibi; tunc tua me infortunia laedent.*[223]

---

[222] John 8:6, 8.

[223] "If you want me to weep, you must first feel grief yourself; then will your misfortunes distress me"; Horace, *Ars Poetica.*

The Perils of the Pinnacle

Apostolic zeal, therefore, is best expressed, not by endlessly talking about the faith, which may sometimes serve only to drive people further away from it, but by living it, by trying to be "other Christs" in the sense of showing forth in the concrete circumstances of our own lives what Christ is like. Needless to say, that does not mean committing the folly and horror of attempting to edify others: it does mean that we should humbly and quietly try, as the prayer in the Mass on the feast of the Ascension tells us, to live in mind and heart among heavenly things.

It also means that we should be very much on our guard against doing harm to others by our example. And it is here again that leaders in the Church have so terrible a responsibility, for things will do harm when done on a pinnacle, especially if the pinnacle is the pinnacle of the temple, which would pass unnoticed in a less exalted position. Christ's ministers or representatives need, more than anyone else, to be meek and humble of heart; if they are to lead others to the temple, they must themselves show their love of the temple by their dignity and reverence; if they are to share in the work of Christ, who came to call sinners, they must share His love of sinners, His patience and gentleness and understanding of human weakness.

We do not think of an outburst of anger as a very dreadful thing when it occurs in ordinary human relationships and is quickly over; it is quite a different matter, however, for a minister of God to display anger, impatience, resentment, or intolerance. Great harm can be done in the confessional by outbursts of harsh invective, and in the Church's juridical processes by a blindness to the pathos of human motivations which, although wrong-headed, can so often have such dignity and loveliness in them. It would be terrible if a priest were to forget that he is supposed to be a father to his flock and became instead a dictator, a feudal lord, a policeman, or a tax-collector. In the days of our Lord, the clerical sins were pride and legalism; it would be more terrible if the same were true of the priests not of the temple but of Christ.

"The hungry sheep look up and are not fed,"[224] wrote Milton: they look up for Christ's food; they look up for His love and understanding and gentleness and encouragement; they look up like the psalmist for His rod for their defense and His staff for their guidance. What an unspeakable tragedy if they were to find none of these things, but only denunciations, incomprehension, prejudice, and a pharisaic zeal to burden others with intolerable obligations. Our Lord spoke of His yoke as sweet and His burden as light:[225] the same could no more be said of Christian legalism and arrogance than it could of pharisaic legalism and arrogance.

But if the pinnacle offers food for thought most obviously to those in high places in Church and society, it has its application also to all Christians. "Do not distress God's Holy Spirit," says St. Paul, "whose seal you bear until the day of your redemption comes."[226] The Church is, in biblical language, a "sealed people": a people set apart, preserved from destruction; and for that very reason, Christians stand out against their pagan or agnostic background.

[224] John Milton, "Lycidas," 1.123.
[225] Matt. 11:30.
[226] Eph. 4:30.

The Perils of the Pinnacle

For the Church makes great claims on man and has momentous things to say about man; and as non-Christians know, She has to stand the searching test laid down in Her own Gospel: "By their fruits you shall know them."[227] The Church is judged largely by the conduct of Her members. In primitive days, the pagans cried out with unwilling admiration: "See how these Christians love one another";[228] in a later day, the cry was repeated, at a time when the still-young Church was torn with savage conflicts and dissensions, and it was repeated no longer in admiration but in scornful irony. In some degree, the reputation of the Church is in the hands of every Christian.

In one of the visions of Ezekiel, we are told how the six angels of destruction were to go forth and smite the city of Jerusalem from end to end because of its iniquities; but beforehand another angel was to mark the brows of all those who bewailed these iniquities, that they might be spared.[229] Again, in Revelation, we read of the four angels at the earth's four corners, holding the winds and ready to unleash them to destroy the earth; but again, there comes first an angel "ascending from the rising of the sun,"[230] who bids them "hurt not

[227] Matt. 7:16, 20.

[228] Tertullian, *Apology*, ch. 39, sect. 7.

[229] Ezek. 9:2-7. The Hebrew text means literally "mark with a *tau*." The *tau* is the last letter of the Hebrew alphabet and means simply a sign or mark of any design: the meaning may be that the brows were to be marked with the letter *tau* itself, which, in the old script, was in the form of a cross.

[230] In Ezekiel's vision, the angels of destruction come from the north gate of the city, the North being always associated with evil and catastrophe; the angel here comes from the East, the source of new life and light, as in Malachi: "Unto you shall the sun of righteousness arise, with healing in his wings (Mal. 4:2)."

the earth, nor the sea, nor the trees" until he has signed the "servants of our God on their foreheads."[231] This idea of signing or sealing is suggested by the signet-ring of the oriental monarch, used for the validation of documents and similar purposes, or again, by the practice of branding slaves and cattle with the owner's mark.

So in both Testaments, the true followers of God are marked as His own, to be preserved from catastrophe. St. Paul has several references to this divine sealing;[232] and St. John speaks of our Lord Himself as sealed by His Father.[233] There are other echoes of the same idea, as when St. Paul speaks of God's foundation-stone standing firm and having on it this seal: "The Lord knoweth who are His";[234] and when, in the primitive Church, the word *seal* is used to mean Baptism and Confirmation. It is against this background, too, that we may read the verse of the Fourth Psalm, as the Vulgate has it: *"Signatum est super nos lumen vultus tui, Domine"*: "The light of Thy countenance, O Lord, is signed upon us: Thou hast given gladness in my heart."[235]

To have the seal is of immense importance to us, for it is our defense against ultimate catastrophe; it is an immense privilege, for it marks us as God's own; it is a thing of gladness, for it is by the Spirit of love and joy that we are sealed. But it also imposes heavy responsibilities: "Do not distress God's

[231] Rev. 7:1-3.
[232] 2 Cor. 1:22; Eph. 1:13, 4:30.
[233] John 6:27.
[234] 2 Tim. 2:19.
[235] Ps. 4:7 (RSV = Ps. 4:6-7).

Holy Spirit: that is the measure of the harm we can do if, having been marked with the seal, we are unfaithful to it.

Can we, in fact, distress God? It certainly would not be true to answer simply no. We can, of course, understand St. Paul as speaking purely metaphorically: attributing distress to God as in other places the Bible speaks metaphorically of His anger or jealousy or repentance. But if we see that and nothing more in what he says, we miss a great deal of its depth and richness. God is utter perfection and happiness and joy; but it was — rather it is — His eternal will that the Word should be made flesh and should share all the suffering and sadness of humanity, and in particular should know the full weight and agony of the world's sin in order to redeem us from it. He suffered in His humanity at a definite point in our world of time, but time is unimportant. He suffered then not merely from the sins of His time or the sins that were past, but from the sins that still lay in the future. So, since the evil we do now caused His suffering then, and since it was God who then suffered, we are right in saying — indeed we are obliged to say — that our sin causes distress to God.[236]

St. Paul, then, is warning us not to take lightly the things that distress God; and it is significant that the warning is preceded and followed by references to sins of speech: "No base talk must cross your lips; only what will serve to build up the faith, and bring a grace to those who are listening. . . . There must be no trace of bitterness among you, of passion, resentment, quarreling, insulting talk, or spite of any kind; be

[236] For a fuller discussion of the sorrow of God, see Gerald Vann, *The Pain of Christ* (London: Blackfriars Publications, 1947), ch. 7.

kind and tender to each other, each of you generous to all, as God in Christ has been generous to you."[237] Why does St. Paul single out these sins as especially distressing to God? We find the answer in St. James: "If anyone deludes himself by thinking he is serving God, when he has not learned to control his tongue, the service he gives is vain."[238]

St. Paul may have had no special need to warn his readers at that time against the more-obvious forms of wrongdoing: they were "sealed with the Holy Spirit" and were perhaps making quite a successful stand against them. But for that very reason they needed to be warned against the sort of sin which is sometimes indulged in by devout people, apparently without any recognition of the fact that they are sinning at all. Sometimes, indeed, they seem to persuade themselves that they are doing something virtuous. They see themselves, and cause others to see them, as impregnable fortresses of virtue, inviolate and incorruptible; and they are filled with an overpowering zeal, not so much to convert their less-happy fellow Christians to better ways, as to confound them and their knavish tricks.

These are the custodians by divine appointment of other people's faith and morals. Like terriers feverishly hunting for lost and buried bones, they are perpetually on the watch for what they regard as error or heresy or evil living; the slightest whiff of heterodoxy goes to their heads like strong wine, and unconventional behavior acts on them like the sting of a hornet. Someone puts forward an opinion which they regard

[237] Eph. 4:29, 31-32 (Knox).
[238] James 1:26 (Knox).

as erroneous or ill-advised; someone else is causing scandal by living in sin of one sort or another: and so the divine afflatus comes upon them, and they give voice.

God gave us the gift of speech so that we might help each other. The tongue is to be used to gladden the heart, as when lovers whisper to each other; it is to be used for blessing — magnificently in the Mass, or humbly when we say to one another, "God bless you"; it is to be used for the healing of the heart in words of comfort, and the healing of the soul in the words of absolution; it is to be used to give courage and strength to the departing soul.

"If anyone deludes himself . . ." The Douay version has "deceiving his own heart." St. James is not warning the manifestly wicked; they can hardly deceive themselves. He is warning those whose outward behavior is in other respects so much above reproach that they may easily deceive themselves: they may fail to see what it really is in their hearts that prompts them to speech; and so they can feel guiltless and, indeed, worthy of high praise, because they never notice the pride, the bitterness, the spite or jealousy, the blindness, the inhumanity, and the pharisaism which really rule them.

There is another phenomenon to be found among modern Catholics that makes St. Paul's admonition particularly opportune today, and that is the widespread inversion of the true scale of values where the relative importance of different virtues and vices is concerned. Perhaps our minds are colored by the Jansenist[239] chapter in our Catholic history; more probably

[239] The morally rigoristic heresy of Jansenism denies the existence of man's free will to accept or reject God's grace.

The Devil

they are colored by the continuance of a Puritan[240] tradition in the non-Catholic society in which we live; or again, it may be that that streak of Manicheism[241] which constantly recurs in Christian history and is to be discerned nowadays in some theological schools and clerical traditions is making its influence felt through pulpit and confessional.[242]

Whatever the explanation, the fact remains: a very large number of modern Catholics seem, in practice, to think that the only sins that really matter are the sensual and, above all, the sexual sins. (To be accurate, one should include with these the sins against the commandments of the Church; for it is common to find Catholics much more concerned about Friday abstinence than about some of the basic commandments of God.) They will be overwhelmed with guilt if they have drunk too much at a party, or fallen in some degree into some sort of carnality; but calumny, backbiting, cruelty, bitterness, arrogance, snobbery, and unalleviated egocentricity they will take cheerfully in their stride, and perhaps be surprised to be told that such things are to be taken seriously. They will

---

[240] The Puritan movement sought to purify the Church of England of all vestiges of Roman Catholicism.

[241] The dualistic heresy of Manicheism teaches that a cosmic conflict exists between a good realm of light and an evil realm of darkness, and that matter belongs to the evil realm.

[242] Perhaps there is some support to be found for this last suggestion in the custom (common among Catholics nowadays in some countries, and presumably due to clerical influence) of talking always of the virtue of purity as "the holy virtue." Certainly God-given purity is holy; but then so are all the other supernatural virtues; and one would have supposed that if any one virtue were to be singled out from all the others in this way, it would be the queen of all the virtues, charity.

even adopt the utterly unchristian habit of using the word *immorality* to mean exclusively sexual immorality.

This is both sad and serious. It is sad because it is the cause, in part, of a tragic amount of sorrow, of real agony of spirit, and sometimes of a discouragement that can lead to despair — all of which is quite unnecessary. Because fallen human nature is what it is, we must expect, unless we are very fortunate and unusual people, to be tempted in one way or another on the sense level, and to be tempted often, perhaps continually, perhaps obsessively. And if that is the case, we must expect also, unless we are very sure of ourselves, that sometimes we shall fail. Now, if these difficulties are seen in their proper perspective, as one element in the totality of the Christian life, they can be dealt with sanely and constructively. When we fall, in this as in any other context, the only reasonable thing is to pick ourselves up again — or rather, to beg God to pick us up again — and to make a fresh start, using our failure as a means to humility and a greater reliance on God, but not at all as an invitation to discouragement or gnawing anxiety.

But if these sins are not one element in a wide and varied struggle, but are the whole struggle, if *immorality* means this and nothing more, then of course failure here will appear as total failure, and the whole life-struggle a total loss. So you find that tragically large numbers of really good people — people filled with the love of God and their fellowmen, sweet and kind and generous and humble — are tortured unbearably in spirit and sometimes brought near to despair because they cannot conquer this one tendency against which they battle bravely, constantly, and often heroically. They will feel they are making no progress at all, are not growing at all in the love of God, because they seem to make no progress in this particular matter; little do they realize that the struggle itself may well involve heroic virtue, and that, in any case, while all this is happening on the surface of the soul, down below in the depths, where faith and hope and love dwell, they are coming closer and closer to the heart of God.

For St. Thomas, and for the great Christian tradition in general, the order of things is quite clear. The gravest sins of all are the sins immediately directed against God: infidelity, for instance, and hatred of God. Next come the grave sins against love of our neighbor: "Six things there are which the Lord hateth, and the seventh His soul detesteth: haughty eyes, a lying tongue, hands that shed innocent blood, a heart that deviseth wicked plots, feet that are swift to run upon a mischievous errand, a deceitful witness that uttereth lies, and him that soweth discord among brethren."[243] There are seven deadly sins, not one; and the one that receives all the attention nowadays is not to be found among these things that the Lord hateth; still less is it the one His soul detesteth.

All this is far from saying that we can treat the sins of the flesh lightly, still less that we can blithely give up the struggle: if we did that, we should very quickly fall into other and greater sins; the whole structure would crumble. But it is essential to keep to the true scale of values: the current situation is serious precisely because, in this sort of obsession with one type of sin, all the others are, in fact, treated lightly — including possibly even those hideous things the Lord hateth, including almost certainly the ugly and very grave things St.

[243] Prov. 6:16-19.

The Perils of the Pinnacle

Paul speaks of. "There must be no trace of bitterness among you, of passion, resentment, quarreling, insulting talk, or spite of any kind; be kind and tender to each other, each of you generous to all, as God in Christ has been generous to you."

"Do not distress God's Holy Spirit": we all need St. Paul's warning; and the more eminent we are, the more urgently we need it, for the pinnacle is a perilous place.

But it can also be, if God so wills, a place of glory. Christ Himself stood there and, in His humility, defeated Satan; and great multitudes of others like Him have since done the same, and are doing the same today. There are all the humble and holy "other Christs" who have done and are still doing such heroic things (at what cost to themselves Christ knows) for the homeless and derelict, the outcasts and criminals, the delinquent children, the Church-haters, and the God-haters, and who, in the end, to their great distress, have been put on the pinnacle of public acclaim. You cannot think of the children of the poor without thinking of Monsieur Vincent de Paul; you cannot think of leper colonies without thinking of Father Damien;[244] to mention the homeless and destitute is to think of men like Abbé Pierre; and from the din of learned psychiatric and legal chatter about cosh-boys and the causes of juvenile delinquency, your thoughts turn gratefully to a Father Flanagan[245] or a Padre Borelli. Men like these find themselves in the end — and usually after years of indifference or opposition or denunciation — put upon a pinnacle,

---

[244] Joseph de Veuster (1840-1889), missionary to leper colonies in the South Pacific.

[245] Edward Joseph Flanagan (1886-1948), founder of Boys Town.

but it harms them no more than it harmed Christ, for they are with Christ.

There is a tradition that it was from the very pinnacle on which Christ stood that St. James the Less[246] was thrown down to death in martyrdom. For it may be a dangerous place in more senses than one, but if it is God's will that a man should stand on it, and if the man is in love with God's will, it must, in the end, lead to everlasting glory.

[246] The Apostle James, son of Alphaeus.

Chapter Six

Presumption and Vainglory

"If Thou be the Son of God, cast Thyself down, for it is written: 'He hath given His angels charge over Thee, and in their hands shall they bear Thee up, lest perhaps Thou dash Thy foot against a stone.' "[247]

For this second temptation, Satan assumes the robes of a divine and carries a Bible: he will show that he, too, can quote the Scriptures. But, as Maldonatus puts it, when our Lord quotes, it is *ut doceat*, to instruct; when Satan quotes, it is *ut decipiat*, to lead astray.

He urges our Lord to cast Himself down. It was what he himself had done: "I saw Satan, like lightning, falling from Heaven"; and in his fall, he involved a host of other angels, as we read in Revelation, in the description of the great red dragon, dragging down with his tail a third part of the stars of heaven and dashing them to earth.[248]

---

[247] Matt. 4:6; Ps. 90:11-12 (RSV = Ps. 91:11-12).
[248] Luke 10:18; Rev. 12:4.

The Devil

Evil suggestions may seem to promise a grand prize, a pinnacle of fame or fortune; but to accept them is to be set on high only to be thrown down lower than we were before. God works with us very differently: if it is His will to exalt a man, He will first of all humble him, for otherwise his exaltation will destroy him. "He has put down the mighty from their seat, and exalted the lowly; He has filled the hungry with good things, and sent the rich away empty-handed."[249]

Satan does not himself cast our Lord down: he must try to persuade Him to do it Himself. That is the limit of his power: he cannot do us spiritual harm except by inducing us to harm ourselves. When he enters into a man, it cannot be by forcing an entry: we have to open the door, to make him welcome. Throwing our Lord down physically would, of course, not have answered his purpose: he is bent on making our Lord sin, and there would be no sin in that. We compass our own downfall.

The psalm quoted by Satan is carefully chosen: it is a psalm of comfort, telling of God's constant care, His power to protect from every danger. "Sheltered under His arms, under His wings, thou art safe; His faithfulness will throw a shield about thee; nothing shalt thou have to fear from nightly terrors, from the arrow that flies by daylight, from trouble that infests the darkness, from the assault of man or fiend under the moon."[250] Let Christ, then, do what He will: no harm can come to Him; angels will attend Him.

In this suggestion there is a double danger. If our Lord acts upon it, He will be guilty of a presumption and vainglory

---

[249] Luke 1:52-53 (Knox).
[250] Ps. 90:4-6 (Knox; RSV = Ps. 91:4-6).

which will lead Him to death; if He refuses, it will perhaps mean a lack of confidence in God.

But if Satan's argument is specious, there are in fact three flaws in it. First, he applies what the psalmist says of the just man, who needs the care of angels to keep him from harm, to our Lord, who does not. The text is not a messianic text. True, the Devil might argue that if God's care is promised to any ordinary just man, it must *a fortiori* be promised to His own Son. But that is a fallacy: the argument from analogy will not hold when there are essential differences instead of an essential resemblance between the two analogues. The angels' protection is promised to the just man and not to the Son of God, not because the Father loves His Son less, but because the Son is in no need of the sort of protection given to the just man.

Secondly, the Devil makes an unwarranted extension of the promise in the psalm: the just man will be guarded against falling into danger; he cannot expect God to protect him if he deliberately puts himself in danger.

Thirdly, as St. Thomas points out, the Devil makes use of the device so often to be met with in controversy, of leaving out anything in the text or context which would tell against him. The psalm goes on to talk of the just man treading safely on asp and adder, and crushing lion and serpent under his feet: and this unfortunate echo of the promise in Genesis that the seed of the woman would crush the serpent's head, and its application to divine protection against temptation itself, is not at all to the Devil's purpose, and is better suppressed.

But why did the Devil hope our Lord would be attracted by the idea of casting Himself down? He would hardly expect Him to be moved simply by vanity to an empty display of power. True, this temptation is traditionally regarded as a temptation to vainglory, but it is not a question of mere vainglory, any more than the first temptation is merely a question of gluttony. Our Lord is clearly not the sort of person to earn a cheap *réclame* by playing to the gallery: He must be tempted, then, in a more spiritual way.

This indeed is Satan's usual technique. When he has to deal with people who have achieved control of their lower appetites and are living good lives, he makes it his object to turn their very goodness, their immunity from the grosser forms of temptation, into another and greater form of temptation. But he will not suggest a blatant form of vanity, any more than he would suggest a blatant form of sensuality. St. Augustine remarks how pride "creeps in stealthily and destroys even good deeds"; and if Satan here is to lure our Lord into pride and presumption, it must be under a cloak of goodness, of some lofty purpose.

That purpose was ready to hand. The sight of our Lord borne up by angels when He cast Himself down from the pinnacle would not only compel the wonder and admiration of the crowd; it would fit in exactly with their conception of what the Messiah was to be, and so it would be easy for Him to compel them to accept Him as their Savior and King. The Gospels give us many indications of what this popular expectation was: the crowds would seek to make Him their king, would distort the meaning of His miracles, would be forever asking for a sign — a sign of the sort they were looking for. They wanted to be dazzled by a display of worldly power; they wanted a political leader who would free them and make them supreme among the nations.

Presumption and Vainglory

And so, as we have seen, the Devil's essential purpose is to cause our Lord to adapt Himself to this popular image of the Messiah and, in this second temptation, to achieve immediate recognition of Himself as the Messiah by a dramatic display of His power. In so doing, He would not only escape all the hardships, the bitterness, the sufferings, and the defeat He would have to encounter along the way mapped out for Him by His Father: He would win the whole people to Him at a single stroke, and He Himself would receive the honor which was, after all, His due. "Father," He was to pray later, "do Thou exalt me at Thy side, in that glory which I had with Thee before the world began";[251] why should He not have something of that glory here and now?

The answer is that we are never to seek glory for ourselves or others unless it is such as will ultimately give glory to God. *Non nobis, Domine, non nobis, sed nomini Tuo da gloriam:* "Not to us, Lord, not to us; but to Thy name give glory."[252] She whose glory was greater than that of any other human creature had said of it, "He that is mighty hath done great things in me, and holy is *His* name."[253] For she saw the glory simply as part of His will. To seek honor for ourselves apart from or in defiance of God's will is not to honor but to dishonor Him.

This would have been the case here, had our Lord sought glory and acclaim by repudiating God's plan for Him. It is a temptation which can come easily to all of us, in various forms, from the petty vanities which lure us into forgetfulness of God

[251] John 17:5.
[252] Ps. 113b:1 (RSV = Ps. 115:1).
[253] Luke 1:49.

to the grandiose pride and ambition which can cause us to defy God. We are not to repudiate glory if it should be God's will for us, any more than we are to try to repudiate the glow of pleasure which must come with any recognition of achievement, any sort of praise or esteem. But applause is heady wine and can easily lead to a purely self-centered pursuit of it. The temptation can sometimes come in subtle form. We write "AMDG"[254] at the top of the pages we write on, and then persuade ourselves that all is well: I bask in the glow of my fame as a great preacher, but of course I am preaching only God and His glory; I achieve great renown as a philanthropist, but was it not Christ Himself who told us that when we feed and clothe His little ones, it is He Himself we feed and clothe?[255]

The Devil did not suggest that our Lord should abandon His interest in God's glory and be concerned only with His own: he suggested that He should seek God's glory by achieving glory Himself. But God is not glorified by any light reflected from us; it is we who, if we do in fact achieve any glory, achieve it by the light reflected from Him.

You may find among Catholics the feeling that luster is shed on the Church by the fact that the great ones of this world are gathered into the fold; and the Catholic press may wax dithyrambic about the reception of a famous novelist or politician or film star into the Church. But if some outstanding personality becomes a Catholic, he does not thereby throw

---

[254] *Ad majorem Dei gloriam* ("for the greater glory of God"), the motto of the Jesuits.

[255] Matt. 25:37-40.

luster on the Church: rather, it is the Church that throws luster on him.

And greatness as the world understands it does not necessarily give glory to God: that is more likely to be done by the little ones who have no truck with human glory. "Not many of you are wise in the world's fashion, not many powerful, not many well-born. No, God has chosen what the world holds foolish, so as to abash the wise; God has chosen what the world holds weak, so as to abash the strong. God has chosen what the world holds base and contemptible, nay, has chosen what is nothing, so as to bring to nothing what is now in being. No human being was to have any ground for boasting, in the presence of God. It is from Him that you take your origin, through Christ Jesus, whom God gave us to be all our wisdom, our justification, our sanctification, and our atonement; so that the Scripture might be fulfilled, 'If anyone boasts, let him make his boast in the Lord.' "[256] It is when the little ones of this world, having no glory of their own, are made glorious by God that His own glory shines out most clearly.

For the most part, we are likely to find that the path marked out for us by God is neither easy nor dramatic, but a matter of quiet plodding along, trying to keep the commandments and to do the work given us to do. Hence the temptation on the one hand to give it a spurious glamour, and on the other to look for shortcuts. For some people, the Gospels and their own God-given reason are not guide enough: they must be looking all the time for private revelations, dramatic manifestations of God's will, or bizarre miracles, or casting about

[256] 1 Cor. 1:26-31 (Knox); Jer. 9:23, 24.

among the more dubious revelations and prophecies of others to throw light on their own lives.

Sometimes it will be the moral life which will seem too drab and laborious: far better to take a shortcut, to forget about the discipline of Christian asceticism, about the Ten Commandments, and to read St. John of the Cross. (But the mystical ladder is not scaled with that ease.) Many devout women (it seems rarely to be the case with men) derive immense satisfaction, and great uplift to the ego, from making something dramatic and extraordinary out of their spiritual lives: they have special difficulties, special graces, and special problems, and they must have special directors with whom they must constantly have long interviews; whereas, in fact, there is nothing about their lives that requires all that particular attention.

Then there are the people for whom the ordinary Christian worship and praise of God is insufficiently glamorous or sentimental. They must do better than that, and so they will have little cults of their own: they will adopt some little-known saint as a sort of private mascot; they will go in for an elaborate and highly emotional cultus of their own devising, and spend far more time and care over some little shrine they have put up to house a secondary relic of a saint than over the altar of God and His tabernacle.

Others will find relief from the boredom and hardship of the service of God in the reward they can derive from the incidentals of that service, as a priest may find food for his vanity in his sacerdotal authority or prestige or panoply, and laypeople may lose sight of the essentials of worship in the satisfaction they derive from its appeal to their senses and feelings.

Presumption and Vainglory

One of the subtler ways in which the temptation to vanity can assail us is under the guise of pure zeal. It is a danger which particularly besets beginners in the spiritual life, such as young religious or recent converts. They have the zest, energy, high spirits, and idealism of youth; the excitement of embarking on a great enterprise; the fervor of a soul freshly and generously given to God. They will not easily be tempted to turn aside from their course until time has brought an abatement of their energy and fervor; and Satan is too shrewd to attempt such a thing. He therefore tries the opposite tactic, of spurring them on, not out of any love of fervor or spiritual endeavor, but because if he cannot quench a flame, his best course is to fan it to the point at which it becomes dangerous.

He will try to turn zeal into rashness, as he tried to turn Christ's trust in His Father into rashness. So he will urge them on to attempt things which are in themselves imprudent or are at least beyond their capacities and so will eventually have to be abandoned, perhaps with a sense of failure or a guilty sense of dereliction of high ideals which will lead to a more general abandonment. They could be doing so much more for God; there are so many activities in which they take no part; they could be devoting more time to prayer; they could be more austere and undertake greater programs of mortification.

So they will try to do more and more; they will wear themselves out in long vigils, and weaken themselves by imprudent ascetical practices; and what was begun in such enthusiasm and high spirits will become an intolerable burden. And then what happens? Either they will contrive somehow to continue their practices, but listlessly and in boredom of spirit, so that their lives become lackluster and somber; or they will give up the struggle altogether, and thereafter find themselves unable or unwilling to undertake even the moderate, reasonable program which spiritual growth demands.

That is why wise directors are at such pains to caution souls against excess; they are attempting, not to dampen the ardors of the zealous soul, but to prevent the tragic consequences of rashness. There is milk for babes and strong meat only for the mature; we must begin in small ways and with the basic things, and make due allowance for our own individual limitations. A wise tradition insists that physical mortification must never be undertaken except under direction because of the obvious dangers there of misguided zeal; but it is not only in that context that zeal can turn into folly or vanity. Prudent and sober counsels may well seem chilly and discouraging to youthful enthusiasm; but the wise director, while explaining the evil effects of indiscreet beginnings, must show that he is trying not to lower the soul's ideals, but to make them attainable.

"Jesus said to him, 'It is written again: "Thou shalt not tempt the Lord thy God." ' "[257] As we have seen, this second temptation is a temptation to both vainglory and presumption: Satan's words primarily suggest thoughts about vainglory; in our Lord's reply, the emphasis is on the element of presumption. He could, of course, have simply pointed out that the Devil had misquoted the text, had misapplied the passage and left out words which were not to his liking. But instead He answers text for text: as Bishop Andrewes[258] put it, the fact

---

[257] Matt. 4:7.

[258] Possibly Lancelot Andrewes (1555-1626), Bishop of Winchester, known especially for his preaching. — ED.

that a wolf can come disguised as a sheep is no reason why the sheep should lay aside its fleece.

And our Lord in His choice of text takes the wise course of going back to general principles concerning our dependence on God's Providence: general principles are always clearer and more certain than particular applications, and particular judgments must always be referred back to them. Satan's use of the Ninetieth Psalm is a misuse because it goes against the general principle that, while we must have confidence in God's care for us, the confidence must never turn into a tempting of God.

To tempt is to test, to put to the proof. St. Thomas points out that we can tempt God either directly, when the words we address to Him or the things we do have as their object to explore His knowledge or power or goodness; or indirectly, when we ask or do something which, in fact, can serve no useful purpose except such an exploration. And he quotes the Gloss[259] on the text quoted by our Lord: He tempts God who, having proper means at his disposal for doing what he had to do, nonetheless exposes himself without reason to danger to see whether God will come to his rescue.[260]

God has appointed certain means for us to use in achieving our purposes. As we learned from the first temptation, we are not to exaggerate their importance or to treat them as all-sufficient. But on the other hand, we are not to ignore or belittle them: they are to be used, and if we fail to make use of them when we can and should, we tempt God.

---

[259] The *Glossa Ordinaria*, the standard medieval commentary on the Bible.

[260] Cf. *Summa Theologica*, II-II, Q. 97, art. 1.

There are circumstances in which ordinary means are lacking, as food and water were lacking to the Israelites in the wilderness, and in such cases, a man must trust God to provide extraordinary means, as He provided the manna and the water from the rock.[261] But only in such cases may we look for such extraordinary help. So our Lord fed His hearers miraculously when He was with them in a desert place and there was no food available by ordinary means,[262] but when they were near a town, they were dismissed to find food for themselves in the ordinary way.[263]

Where there is a real need, God will not forsake us: that is the meaning of the Ninetieth Psalm. The dangers from which the angels will protect the just are dangers against which there is no natural escape, evils which no reasonable care or foresight can avert. The snare of the hunter, the arrow that flies by day, the pestilence that infests the darkness: these are symbols of such evils, for the snare is hidden, the arrow comes swiftly from afar, and the pestilence hides under the darkness. But where ordinary means are available and sufficient, we are not to expect miracles. St. Paul tells us, "If a man will not work, neither let him eat."[264] If our Lord wishes to descend from the temple roof, He must walk down the steps.

In temporal affairs, men are not likely, for the most part, to despise or neglect the ordinary, natural ways of satisfying their needs, of finding food and drink, clothing, shelter, and the

---

[261] Deut. 8:15-16.
[262] Matt. 14:15-20; Mark 6:35-42; Luke 9:12-17.
[263] John 4:8.
[264] 2 Thess. 3:10.

amenities of life; they are more likely to be too wrapped up in such pursuits. But it is not always so among pious people. Perhaps it is a misunderstanding of St. Paul's "the grace of God is sufficient"[265] that leads them to act as they do; perhaps it is a kind of pride which leads them to think of ordinary ways and means as beneath the notice of elect souls; perhaps it is just plain dullness of wit.

The fact remains that you will find people who, when they become low in health or in spirits from misguided and excessive ascetical practices, will not stoop to take the rest and relaxation which prudence would exact to remedy the state of affairs, but will, on the contrary, resort to yet more intensive prayer and fasting, so that they soon become not better but worse. In asceticism itself, you will come across unhealthy practices deriving from an unhealthy theory: that the goodness of actions is to be assessed by the difficulty or unpleasantness which the actions involve. Those who hold this view think that the way to perfection, therefore, lies in going against nature as much as possible: do penance with savage intensity even though it ruins your health; never allow yourself any relaxation — is not idleness a sin? — even though you become a neurotic; if you are ill, have no truck with doctors and medicines, but accept it all as a welcome cross or simply resort to prayer; leave the cult of what is reasonable to the pagan philosophers, and follow the gospel of rigid opposition to what is natural.

For St. Thomas, grace is not at a tangent to nature: it works in and through nature. If a room is to be swept for God's greater

---

[265] Cf. 2 Cor. 12:9.

glory, it must be swept with a broom, not a litany. A mood of sadness, St. Thomas suggests, is to be cured by sleep and a good, hot bath.[266] Right action is action that is reasonable; and to think that we can live for God by despising our God-given reason is not only presumption, but something approaching blasphemy.

Where spiritual things are concerned, it is all too easy to think we can bypass ordinary means, that we can attain holiness without ordinary discipline. There are many rungs on the ladder to Heaven, and each has to be tackled. It would be presumption to suppose that we need not bother our heads about commandments and prohibitions, about exhortations to virtue and the avoidance of vice; to suppose that we can forget all about that and enjoy life, that it will be time enough for all that when death is near, for God is merciful, and when that time comes, we can throw ourselves on His mercy. No, we are to take all that the Ninetieth Psalm offers us of comfort, of confidence in God's care and protection, but to take it as a guarantee, not that all will be well in the end no matter what we do or fail to do now, but that all will be well provided we constantly turn here and now to that loving care as the source of the strength we need, all the days of our lives, to serve Him faithfully.

This is made clear in the continuation of the text quoted by our Lord: "Thou shalt not put the Lord thy God to the proof, as thou didst at the Place of Challenge; it is for thee to live by His commandments, by the decrees and observances He has enjoined on thee, to obey the Lord's good pleasure. So

---

[266] *Summa Theologica*, I-II, Q. 38, art. 5.

shalt thou prosper, and the fair land which the Lord promised to thy fathers shalt be thine to have and to hold."[267]

Balaam prayed that his soul might die the death of the just and his end be like theirs:[268] that is what we all wish for, but the appointed way to come by such a death is to live the life of the just. And Ecclesiastes bids us not put off until old age the attempt to serve God: "Remember thy Creator in the days of thy youth, before the time of affliction comes, and the years draw nigh of which thou wilt say: 'They please me not.' "[269] Here and now, flesh lusts against spirit and spirit against flesh, and we have to struggle to establish harmony between them, to learn self-control; here and now, we have to watch and pray that we enter not into temptation; here and now, we have to learn to live with God in prayer lest death come upon us with the lesson still unlearned. Balaam saddled his ass and set forth on his journey unaware of the fact that God was angry at his going. He felt secure, and jogged along happily, and so would have run onto the angel's sword if the ass had not been less blind than he.[270] We too can have a feeling of security which is, in fact, false security, if we misunderstand God's mercy and think that some miracle will save us no matter what we do.

We are not, of course, to put a limit on God's power or mercy: it may be that He is merciful to us even in our presumption, and will give us grace to accomplish in some extraordinary way what we could have accomplished, but for our folly,

---

[267] Deut. 6:16-18.
[268] Num. 23:10.
[269] Eccles. 12:1.
[270] Num. 22:21-23.

in ordinary ways. But it is no part of His promises that He will do so, and we are not to expect it. On the contrary, there is every reason to fear He will not, for in rejecting ordinary means, we have already, in a sense, rejected His Providence, since they are precisely the design of that Providence for us and the gift of His mercy.

Another way in which we can fall into presumption is by pinning our hopes unduly on good works: "I can't keep the Commandments, but I do quite a lot of good in the world, so all will be well." There is a dangerous fallacy here, for it is possible to do good to other people without doing oneself any good. A man may think his labors for others must be sufficient to save him no matter how deplorable his own personal life may be; but although they are good works in the sense of doing good to others, they may not be good in the sense of being done for the love of God. Such a life could be no more than the fulfilling of selfish ambitions and greeds.

Another man may comfort himself by reflecting that, in spite of all his sins, there is hope for him since he is at least a kindly person, always doing good turns for others; after all, he has read that charity covers a multitude of sins.[271] But his kindness may be a purely natural characteristic; he may enjoy being kind; he may be kind because of the popularity his kindness brings him or because being a benefactor ministers to his sense of power; and none of that is charity.

In a sermon on Esau and Jacob, St. Augustine treats of them as symbols, the former of carnal men, the latter of spiritual men. And he points out that while they have in common, in

[271] 1 Peter 4:8.

their father's blessing, the prayer that God may give them dew from heaven and fruitful soil, it is Jacob who is promised lordship over his brethren, that they shall serve him, whereas Esau is told that he will be subject to his brother.[272] For the carnal serve the spiritual, perhaps by actual ministrations, but at least by giving them occasion to grow in patience and tolerance; and thus they profit the spiritual although not themselves. If we cause ourselves, because of our misdeeds, to be ranked among the carnal, we may still serve Jacob and yet have no grounds for any feeling of security on that account. It must be added, though, that Esau in his blessing was promised servitude only until he should shake off the yoke; for he, too, was given the dew of heaven and the fruitful soil — the word of God and the visible sacraments — and if the carnal man makes use of these, he may free himself from the yoke of sin and be numbered among the spiritual. Until then, it must remain true that any feeling of confidence would be presumption.

The same holds good of the externals of religious obser-vance. It would be very foolish to say, "I go to church every morning, I am always at Benediction, I belong to all of the parochial guilds and sodalities, and therefore my place in Heaven is assured." As William Law[273] pointed out, it is possi-ble to use the "outward forms and modes of religion [to] keep all things quiet in us" — to avoid thinking, to avoid the discomfort of a direct contact with God and the challenge which it would involve. It is possible also to pervert the nature of these observances: to make them not acts of worship, but

[272] Gen. 27:28-29, 39-40.
[273] British spiritual writer (1686-1761).

forms of self-indulgence. It is possible to become a "pillar of the parish" not because you love God, but because you enjoy being a pillar.

The Israelites, St. Paul tells us, hoped to be justified but were not because "they hoped to derive their justification from observance, not from faith";[274] and again, he says of Abraham and his posterity that "it was not through obedience to the law, but through faith justifying them" that they were promised the inheritance of the world.[275] By "the law," he means here the observances of the Old Law, but it is not inadmissible to apply his words to observances under the new dispensation, and to "works" in general as opposed to faith, to that loving faith which alone gives them supernatural value.

The idea that we can buy God's blessing and our own salvation dies hard, but it is equally invalid whether we think of the purchase price in terms of vast sums of money willed for posthumous Masses or of ostentatious philanthropies or of a fine showing in terms of pious observances and parochial activities.

It is doubtless a perception of this basic truth which has given the idea of being *dans les oeuvres*[276] such a pejorative color in French: for the picture that the phrase conjures up is that of a hard-lipped, domineering, self-righteous woman, the self-constituted right hand of the *curé* in his battle against wrongdoing, a woman whose "charities" give her the right and the opportunity to upbraid or bully or patronize the recipients

[274] Rom. 9:32 (Knox).
[275] Rom. 4:13 (Knox).
[276] "In the works": devoted to good works.

of them, and who convinces herself that she is securing her own right of entry into Heaven by making life on earth a hell for everyone who is unfortunate enough to come under her dominance.

It is not the blood of calves and goats, still less the blood of human hearts, that will render us acceptable to the Lord, no matter how piously we set about our sacrificial rites;[277] there is relevance here in the words of Ezekiel: "I will take away from your breasts those hearts that are hard as stone, and give you human hearts instead,"[278] for the sacrifice God loves is an afflicted spirit; it is only the heart that is "contrite and humbled" that He will not despise.[279]

All that, however, should not lead us to minimize the value of works which are really good, which have in them the love of God and of man. Charity does indeed cover a multitude of sins, and many sins were forgiven Mary Magdalene because she loved much.[280] The priest who faithfully, humbly, patiently serves his flock may surely hope with confidence for the mercy of God even though his own personal faults are many; the same is true of the layman or woman who, in spite of many difficulties, remains doggedly faithful to the Mass, to prayer, and to the life of charity. And if there are men and women for whom "good works" are an excuse for thrusting themselves forward, for interfering with other people's lives, or for slaking their thirst for power, there are many others who, without any

[277] Cf. Heb. 10:4.
[278] Ezek. 36:26 (Knox).
[279] Ps. 50:19 (RSV = Ps. 51:17).
[280] Luke 7:47.

self-importance whatsoever, are always humbly and selflessly ready to answer a call for help from their priests, their friends, and their next-door neighbors; and that sort of charity, while it is compatible with many failings, must surely outweigh them all in the eyes of God.

Chapter Seven

Pride or Freedom

"Again the Devil took Him up into a very high mountain, and shewed Him all the kingdoms of the world, and the glory of them."[281]

Again: the word is important. Just as we have to be importunate in prayer, like the man in the parable who, by his persistence, finally induced his friend to get up in the middle of the night and lend him bread,[282] so we have to expect that Satan will be importunate in tempting us. To return to the attack after one repulse would show a certain determination, but he returns again and again; even when this third attack is repulsed, he retires, as St. Luke tells us, only for a time.[283]

It is not enough, then, to prevail two or three times against temptation in order to feel secure. Any such feeling of security would be a dangerous thing, for it would be a false security. The

---

[281] Matt. 4:8.
[282] Luke 11:5-8.
[283] Luke 4:13.

Devil is not easily discouraged; on the contrary, resistance is a challenge to him, and he will go on in the hope of wearying us in the end, as Delilah wearied Samson, "plying him with questions day after day, and giving him no peace, until at last she crushed his spirit altogether, and made life a burden to him; and at last he told her the truth."[284]

It is sometimes cynically said that good people owe their virtue simply to the fact that they have never been tempted. The opposite is more likely to be true, for as we have seen, only if we resist temptation are we likely to know its full force; the man who gives way at once may not even realize he has been tempted. As St. John Chrysostom says, "He goes into the desert who goes forth from the city, the will of the flesh and the world, where temptation has no place; for who would be tempted to unlawful lust who all day long was with his wife?"[285] No, resistance will not gain us a final freedom from attack. Satan is sometimes called Beelzebub, the "Lord of Flies": you wave a fly away, but again and again it comes back, and Satan has the same persistence.

This third attack is more open than the others. In the first place, he came feigning sympathy for our Lord in His hunger; next he pretended to want to help to promote our Lord's work, and offered a suggestion as to how that work might be done more quickly and brilliantly. But now he casts off all pretense; he appears in his own character as Prince of this world. And like a prince, he will not bargain. He offers all he has (and his possessions are princely indeed) to induce our Lord to commit

[284] Judg. 16:16 (Knox).
[285] Quoted by St. Thomas Aquinas, *Commentary on Matthew*, ch. 4.

one sin. One sin only — but it would have brought about the defeat of all mankind.

He takes our Lord up into a very high mountain, for he wants Him to see with His own eyes all the kingdoms of the world. We are more easily moved, solicited, by what we see than by what we merely hear about. Modern salesmen know that to induce a customer to look at their wares is to lower their sales-resistance. So it was that Satan dealt with Eve, first showing her how the fruit was "fair to the eyes and delightful to behold" so that then she took and ate it and gave it to her husband.[286] Again, we are told that the corruption which brought about the deluge was due to the fact that the sons of God saw and lusted after the beauty of the daughters of men;[287] and David's passion, which led him to murder, was roused by the sight of Bathsheba.[288]

That is why we find it so much harder to love spiritual realities, the invisible things of God, than the things which are visible to our bodily eyes and delightful to behold. It is not sinful to look at the beauty of created things — on the contrary, we are to praise and thank God for them; to despise them would be to despise their Maker — but it can be dangerous for those who have not achieved self-mastery. Lot and his wife were forbidden to look back as they fled from Sodom,[289] but Abraham was left free, being a man whose passions were under control; and our Lord reminds us of the fate of Lot's wife when

[286] Gen. 3:6.
[287] Gen. 6:2.
[288] 2 Kings 11:2-3, 15 (RSV = 2 Sam. 11:2-3, 15).
[289] Gen. 19:17.

telling us not to make perishable things our main concern and warning us that if we want to find life, we must first of all lose it, lest like those men of old, we should eat and drink, buy and sell, plant and build, only in the end to be destroyed.[290]

It was all the kingdoms of the world that Christ was to see and be offered: unlimited wealth and power and glory. The bait must surely be difficult to resist, for the desire of these things and the satisfactions they can bring is very strong in mankind. Just as Lucifer was not content to be less than God, so Eve was not content to be mistress of the world, but attempted to climb higher. The world's history is full of the damage done by greed and ambition and the lust for power. Sometimes these urges are overt and obvious to everyone, as with the politician who will give anything for political power, or the social climber, or the neurotic sufferer from mild delusions of grandeur. Sometimes they are submerged, and appear only in the form of bitterness, hostility, and criticism of those who are in possession and enjoyment of the coveted prize.

The competitive spirit and the evils to which it gives rise loom particularly large in our culture today. "Sociologists and psychologists have commented much upon the importance of the role of competition in our society. The basic reason for this exaggeration is generally asserted to be economic, for in our economic structure, everything is based upon the principle of individual competition. From the field of economics this competitive attitude extends itself to other and, perhaps, to all other aspects of life. The individual learns to see that in order to be secure and to make his way successfully, it is necessary

[290] Luke 17:32-33, 28-29.

to match himself against other individuals, to surpass them in excellence and accomplishment or in prestige, to dominate and control them, and possibly to bring about their defeat as real or at least potential threats to his own security or advantage. And his habit of looking upon others in this way, together with the hostile tension it implies, has an unfortunate tendency to pervade and color all his human relationships."[291]

This sort of urge, derived from a secular environment, may well make itself felt in the sphere of religion, not so much perhaps in the form of "conscious and deliberate inclinations" as in the form of "emotional predispositions and tendencies." If a boy learns to feel that he must at all costs be "stronger, more dominant, more loved, more gifted or admired than his fellows," then the urge to achieve that sort of excellence will not be likely to be wholly absent from his religious strivings. "On the contrary, it will continue to spur him on and will manifest itself in strong tendencies to pride, vanity, envy, jealousy, obstinacy, and the like, depending upon circumstances and the peculiar bent and direction of his habitual attitudes."[292]

So he will not want to rest content with the ordinary virtues, the ordinary piety, and the ordinary prayers and religious practices of his fellow Christians. He will always want to go one better than his neighbor; and so he will act on the assumption that the more pedestrian aspects of the Christian life are the proper and indeed the only way for dullards, but

[291] P. K. Meagher, "The Spirit of Religious Obedience in Modern America," *Men's Religious Community Life in the United States* (New York: Paulist Press, 1952), 191-192.

[292] Ibid., 192.

not at all the way for chosen souls such as he. For them, the Our Father will suffice: it is all they can manage. But for him is the prayer of union, the mystical marriage. That sort of assumption is folly; for we never outgrow the Our Father any more than we outgrow the Ten Commandments; and to attempt to scale the mystical heights while scorning these simple but essential things would be to invite a fall indeed.

The urge to excel, to exalt ourselves in one way or another, must clearly make the humble way of the Christian very hard; and we need to be very much on our guard against it.

Not that it is anything new. We meet it in the Gospels, when the wife of Zebedee can think of nothing better to ask of Christ for her sons than that they shall sit one at His right hand and the other at His left when He comes into His kingdom;[293] and this attitude of mind seems to be shared to some extent by others of the apostolic group who cling to the idea that the kingdom of Israel, as they understand it, will be restored and that they themselves will then be glorified.[294] We meet it in the Old Testament, as in the story of Balaam, who, at first, resisted the Moabite king's attempts to bribe him to come and curse the Israelites. But later, when Balac persisted and offered him all the wealth and honors he could wish, Balaam found the bait too alluring to be refused and, as St. Peter says, "was content to take pay in the cause of wrong, and was rebuked for his perversity when the dumb beast spoke with a human voice to bring a prophet to his senses."[295]

[293] Matt. 20:20-21.
[294] Acts 1:6.
[295] 2 Peter 2:15-16 (Knox); cf. Num. 22:28.

We can understand the appeal of avarice and ambition — we who in one form or another feel the tug of them. But we might wonder what there was in the Devil's suggestion which could be expected to win over this man who had shown Himself so free from the tyranny of material things and from vanity, so dedicated to God.

We can find the answer in the difference between the temptation which our Lord resisted and the temptation to which Faust succumbed. Both are offered the kingdoms of the world and, as St. Luke significantly adds, the glory of them, but under quite different aspects. Faust is, on a grand scale, what most of us are in smaller ways. He is the symbol of human greed, of the lust for money or pleasure or power, grown so imperative as to make a man ready to pay any price, even his own soul, if his greeds can be satisfied. The bait in his case, then, is power in itself, and the pleasures that power can provide.

But in our Lord's case, it is much more than that. Satan is saying in effect, "Accept me as Your overlord, and I shall put no obstacle in the way of the spread of Your kingdom; more than that, I shall show You how to win the whole world, and win it easily and finally. Reject the way I offer You, and You will fail, and Your work will be a failure: You will win over a fraction of humanity, no more, and them You will condemn to hardship and misery."

As Lagrange points out, the *idée maîtresse* of the three temptations as a whole is that victory must come from God alone in accordance with His will, without any attempt to escape from it or to do violence to it, and this will was that Satan should be conquered by patience and humility, not by power.[296] Men, too, must be won by patience and humility, not by power. The way of power would destroy their freedom, and what God demands of them is love, and love can only be given freely.

Yet how strong a case can be put, as Dostoyevsky's Grand Inquisitor put it, for the folly of the way of freedom: "Thou wouldst go into the world, and art going with empty hands, with some promise of freedom which men in their simplicity and their natural unruliness cannot even understand, which they fear and dread — for nothing has ever been more insupportable for a man and a human society than freedom. But seest thou these stones in this parched and barren wilderness? Turn them into bread, and mankind will run after thee like a flock of sheep, grateful and obedient." But He would not; just as He would not cast Himself down from the temple, and would not come down from the Cross when they called to Him to do so, for "thou didst crave for free love and not the base raptures of the slave before the might that has overawed him forever. But thou didst think too highly of men therein, for they are slaves, of course, though rebellious by nature." He refused, just as He refused "the world and Caesar's purple"; "hadst thou accepted that last counsel of the mighty spirit, thou wouldst have accomplished all that man seeks on earth — that is, someone to worship, someone to keep his conscience, and some means of uniting all in one unanimous and harmonious ant heap, for the craving for universal unity is the third and last anguish of man."[297]

---

[296] *Saint Matthew*, 64.
[297] Fyodor Dostoyevsky, *The Brothers Karamazov*, Bk. 5, ch. 5.

"Traham omnia ad me," He was to say: He would draw all creatures to Him;[298] but He would draw them with a Cross, not a crown. For the service of God is the "freedom of the sons of God";[299] it is the service of Satan that is a slavery. The winning of the whole world by power-means would have meant worshiping Satan, because it would have meant that degradation of man which is Satan's purpose. There is such a thing as the worship of Satan in a direct and personal sense; but what is much more common and therefore more important for humanity as a whole is the indirect worship of Satan in the sense of selling oneself into the slavery of evil — of choosing evil ends or, more subtly, of choosing evil means to good ends. Perhaps we shall bring home to ourselves the full force of this third temptation and its relevance to our own lives if we view it in that light.

There is no lack in the Church's history of pages in which this sort of temptation triumphs. There have been mass conversions brought about, not by Christ's Cross, but by Caesar's purple and Caesar's sword. There are all the examples of heretics brought to retract their errors by unendurable torture. The story of the Crusades is not a wholly edifying story.

But we need not search the past for examples of this sort of thing. Cruelty and violence are not the only forms of the use of power-means. As we have already noted, you will find well-intentioned but foolish parents who, in their determination to make their children follow some particular vocation, go far beyond the legitimate bounds of parental guidance, and

[298] Cf. John 12:32.
[299] Rom. 8:21.

sweeping aside all consideration of their children's aptitudes and leanings, will endeavor to persuade them that this life is the obvious one for them, so that the children follow what is, in fact, a false vocation, and perhaps end in utter catastrophe. You will come across the cult of ignorance in the name of innocence: withholding knowledge because knowledge is dangerous. You will find theology being turned from a vital and ever-evolving search for deeper insights into the truth to a dull, rigid, doctrinaire *ipse dixit*. The fear-motive and the negativism which springs from it, both so pervasive in modern Catholicism, are examples of the same sort of thing: expressed as they are in the constant emphasis on what is to be shunned rather than on what is to do, and in the curbing of initiative in the interests of safety.

But we would be wrong to suppose that if we are lowly and unimportant and without power, this temptation cannot apply to us. To Christ, the Devil offered all the kingdoms of the world and their glory; with us, he can be content with something far less grandiose to achieve his purposes. A very tiny kingdom, a mere hint of glory, may suffice. Every man has his price, the cynic declares; it may be that ours is not very high. Perhaps the Devil will not need to take us up into a mountain; perhaps a molehill will be eminence enough from which to arouse our petty greeds. And he need not say, "All these will I give thee," but just, "This will I give thee" — and we are ready to adore Satan, to make evil our master.

Nor should we be blind to the ingenuity with which otherwise good people will salve their consciences by finding excuses for sharp practice of one sort or another where their interests demand it. If we steal, we say that the sum is so small as to be negligible, or that, after all, only the government will suffer, or that it is for a good cause. If we cheat or defraud or trick somebody, we may call it legitimate business enterprise. People will make use of their friends in the most shameless way, will enjoy to the full the sweets of spiteful tittle-tattle, will make small adjustments in their accounts, will lie un-blushingly, will devote their lives with a sort of epic single-mindedness to the pleasures of the table, or will calmly sit in judgment on their neighbors, apparently without any suspi-cion that there is anything amiss; what they have seen from their molehill has filled their whole horizon, and they are quite unaware of Satan standing close behind them.

That is perhaps the main danger when our temptations are on a small scale; we may not even realize that we are being tempted. In religious life, obedience will sometimes impose a great and unpleasant change of circumstances which, because it is great, is a challenge: it may well bring out the best in a man, but at least its relation to obedience cannot pass unno-ticed. But the small everyday trials and irritations which obe-dience brings in its train may come to be regarded simply as trials and not as duties at all, and so they may be shirked, or else accepted only with grumbling and rancor, without any stirrings of conscience.

The same is true of the moral life generally. If some big issue is at stake and the issue is clear, perhaps we shall find strength to do what is right; whereas in small matters we may be careless, may not notice we are doing evil, and so little by little may be led, as David was led, from small transgressions to greater. So it was, too, with Peter in his cowardice; he began by following afar off, then denied that he was a follower of our

The Devil

Lord, and finally was led into declaring with oaths that he knew not the Man.[300]

Satan's implication in this third temptation, as in the first, is that God is a poor provider, that He offers a meager reward for faithful service: it is to Satan himself that we must look if we want prosperity and glory. And on a very short-sighted view, there is truth in the contention. As the psalmist observed, it is the wicked who prosper and grow rich, whereas the reward of the righteous in this world is often only poverty and affliction.[301] So it is easy to weary in well-doing, and then to fall an easy prey to some glittering offer from Satan.

We do well to take a longer view. Satan promised our Lord the kingdoms of the world if He would *fall down* and adore him: the bait is eminence, excellence, and glory, but the actual result is degradation. In the same way, he promised the first human beings that they would be as gods; whereas, in fact, they became like "the beasts that perish."[302] The service of God, on the other hand, may seem to offer only hard and lowly things, but they lead in the end to glory. So a great man, in a moment of extreme national peril, offers his countrymen only "blood, tears, toil, and sweat";[303] but he leads them thereby to "their finest hour."[304] To gain the Devil's prizes, we must grovel; but if we go to God, we must keep our heads high: we must climb steps to enter the church and, once inside, must raise

[300] Matt. 26:58, 69-72; Mark 14:54, 66-71.
[301] Ps. 72:12-14 (RSV = Ps. 73:12-14).
[302] Ps. 48:13 (RSV = Ps. 49:12).
[303] Winston Churchill, speech, *Hansard*, 13 May 1940, col. 1502.
[304] Churchill, speech, *Hansard*, 18 June 1940, col. 60.

our eyes to the altar, to the East, to the rising of the sun: "I lift up my eyes to the hills, to find deliverance; from the Lord deliverance comes to me, the Lord who made Heaven and earth."[305]

Heaven and earth: the earth and its fullness is not Satan's but the Lord's.[306] Satan is indeed the Prince of this world, but it is the world in the Gospel sense: the world of darkness, of evil, of emptiness. For evil is nonbeing. True, the evils we choose are positive enough; but they are positive only insofar as there is goodness — reality — in them. Just as Satan is still an angel, but a warped, twisted angel, so our lusts are a dark perversion of something radiant. Just as hatred is the blackness of a withered heart, so anger is a dark fire, and cruelty is power turned to darkness, and avarice and proud ambition are dark, devouring cankers.

William Law was fond of contrasting the dark fire with the Fire which is Light. The latter burns away all dross, all evil, until the soul is incandescent, able to join the Light in fullness of being; the former burns away all gold, all goodness, until the soul is empty, sunk in nothingness. Satan's gifts pervert the whole order of creation, for whereas God made being out of nothingness and light out of darkness, Satan turns being into nothingness and light into darkness; so, too, the price to be paid for his gifts is a perversion of the whole relationship of creature to Creator, for instead of worshiping the Light, we must worship the Darkness. It is not surprising if, in our Lord's final words, there is a note of anger and indignation: "Begone,

[305] Ps. 120:1 (Knox; RSV = Ps. 121:1-2).
[306] Ps. 23:1 (RSV = Ps. 24:1).

The Devil

Satan: for it is written, 'The Lord thy God shalt thou adore, and Him only shalt thou serve.' "[307]

Christ had suffered the other temptations patiently, but here it is different. For the other temptations were an affront to Him as Messiah: this one is an affront to the Godhead, since its aim is to divert to the Devil the glory due to God, which is the most infamous perversion conceivable. Hence our Lord is roused to anger here as He was roused to anger at the defilement of God's temple,[308] and as Moses — a meek man above all the men of the earth — had been roused to anger at the idolatry of his people.[309] It is wrong to lose one's temper, but it can be wrong also not to be angry.[310]

Our Lord might have disputed Satan's claim to have it in his power to give Him all the kingdoms of the earth; He might have pointed out that his word was not to be relied on — had he not promised Adam and Eve that they would be as gods? Instead He chooses a text which shows clearly the enormity of the Devil's suggestion. Even if Satan had the power he claimed, and even if his word could be relied on, still the suggestion could not be entertained for a moment: it is God whom we are to adore, Him only whom we are to serve. The

[307] Matt. 4:10.

[308] Matt. 21:12-13.

[309] Num. 12:3; Exod. 32:19.

[310] The anger, to be a just anger, must be under the control of reason all the time, and therefore it is easy for us to sin by excess, to allow the anger to get out of hand; but to fail to be angered by such things as blasphemous insults to God or diabolical cruelty to men is to sin by defect, for it argues either a very unworthy weakness and lack of spirit or else the sort of "tolerance" which is, in fact, a complete lack of principle or moral sense.

only is important: Satan would be willing to admit that God is to be served provided that he were served also, but God will not accept a partial allegiance; as our Lord was to say later on, we cannot serve both God and mammon.[311]

Yet how readily, in practice, we try to do so!

We worship God, we pray to Him, and sometimes we obey Him; but at other times, we obey very different gods of our own choosing, and in so doing, we repudiate the one God. For God will have no partner; if we attempt to put Him in a pantheon, to make Him one of many whom we serve, or even one of two, then we fail to see Him as He is. He is not one of many or even one of two: He is *the Lord God*, and there is no other: He made the heavens and the earth, and the issue of all things is in His hands alone. If, in our pride, avarice, ambition, and lust, we kneel before the Devil, if we divide the glory, then God is lost to us.

Satan has no need to offer us all the kingdoms of the earth: something much more modest is quite enough to inflame our lust for power or pleasure, and we snatch eagerly at the prize, not caring about the implications of what we are doing. Many an apostasy, one must suppose, has been due to the love of money or power, or of a human being, or due to pride or the lust for pleasure. But we need not think only of such dramatic examples. We should think, too, of the smaller compromises we make in our allegiance to God: the ways in which, for the sake of some worldly advantage or the avoidance of some worldly loss or embarrassment, we will conceal our religious allegiance or at least make others think that we treat it very

[311] Matt. 6:24; Luke 16:13.

The Devil

lightly, or again, we will forget the demands of charity or even justice. And all this is, in fact, to fall down and do the Devil's bidding.

"And the Devil left Him." It is not suggested that he went willingly — "Begone": he was dismissed; and we can take comfort from that fact. We are not to suppose that the Devil is allowed to attack us, to molest us, just as he pleases. On the contrary, God "will not allow us to be tempted beyond our strength."[312] He does not altogether spare us the trial, but He checks and restrains the tempter, so that the temptation itself may become in the end a good rather than an evil experience. He could, of course, make things easier for us, shield us from every attack, and that would indeed be a mercy; but it is a greater mercy to suffer us to be tempted while ensuring that by His grace, we come through the ordeal unhurt. For "endurance gives proof of our faith, and a proved faith gives ground for hope. Nor does this hope delude us."[313]

"Then the Devil left Him; and behold angels came and ministered to Him."[314] Even now our Lord is patient: He waits for the angels to minister to Him, and in God's good time, they come. That is often the order of things in the ways marked out for us by God: first the trials, the sufferings, and the difficult things, and afterward comfort, joy, and peace. "Lord, Thou hast put us to the proof," writes the psalmist, "tested us as men test silver in the fire; led us into a snare, and bowed our backs with trouble, while human masters rode us down; our way led

[312] 1 Cor. 10:13.
[313] Rom. 5:4-5 (Knox).
[314] Matt. 4:11.

through fire and water, but now Thou hast brought us out into a place of repose."³¹⁵

With the Devil, it is the other way around: first the allurements, the tree "fair to the eye and delightful to behold,"³¹⁶ and the fleeting moment of contentment, but then the sense of guilt, loss, remorse, and disintegration. And how little we learn by experience! Not only do we go on persuading ourselves that in the Devil's gifts our true happiness is to be found, but also we go on blandly ignoring his power, so that we play into his hand by recklessly putting ourselves into circumstances which we know to be perilous for us.

Do you believe in the Devil?

It is clear that our Lord accepted not merely the fact of his existence but his might, his terrible power to harm, to warp the world. "I saw Satan, like lightning, falling from Heaven":³¹⁷ the blaze, the terror, but also the beauty, a beauty dark and distorted but beauty nonetheless. For this, once again, is neither the gnostics' evil-in-itself nor the little red demon of medieval imagery, but the mighty spirit who has devoted his radiance to the working of evil. Swinburne was being childish when he wrote of the "lilies and languors of virtue, the raptures and roses of vice,"³¹⁸ but vice has nonetheless an allurement which is like a reflection of that satanic radiance.

Angels came and ministered to Him. They came when the ordeal was over; for He who had power to summon legions of

---

³¹⁵ Ps. 65:10-12 (Knox; RSV = Ps. 66:10-12).

³¹⁶ Gen. 3:6.

³¹⁷ Luke 10:18.

³¹⁸ Algernon Charles Swinburne, "Dolores," stanza 9.

The Devil

angels had power also to dismiss the Devil when He would. With us in our frailty, it is very different; and we should be well-advised, as soon as temptation comes upon us, to invoke those other mighty spirits whose purpose is not to harm but to help mankind.

But it is not enough merely to pray for help at the time of temptation: there must also be the continuous struggle to grow in strength by growing in love, and to come closer to God by prayer. St. Paul tells us: "You must hold what is evil in abomination, fix all your desire upon what is good."[319] We can all manage to hate some forms of evil and to love some forms of goodness, but that is not enough: we are to learn to hate *everything* evil and to love *everything* good. The man who succeeds in doing that is indeed armed against temptation, for there is in him then what St. Thomas calls a connaturality with the good and an instinctive revulsion against evil. That is what we have to pray for and, with God's grace, attempt to achieve.

The angels came and ministered to Christ's bodily needs: they brought Him bread, renewed His strength. And we, for our part, are taught that if we pray for strength, it will not be denied us; that if we ask our heavenly Father for bread, He will not give us a stone.[320] In fact, God's supremely strengthening gift, the eucharistic Bread, is daily offered to us; and when we go down from the altar, back to the world where so many temptations await us, we go armed against them because of the power the Bread has given us.

[319] Rom. 12:9.
[320] Cf. Matt. 7:9, 11.

And in that power is freedom. If we are proud and refuse to ask God's help, we fall inevitably into slavery, into the power of Satan. If we keep our eyes steadfastly on the mountain whence help comes to us, being constant in prayer and above all constant and fervent in our approach to the altar, then we can hope to find freedom, the freedom of the sons of God. And so we can come in the end to possess some share of that power and that quiet assurance of which St. Paul speaks when he tells us: "I can do all things in Him who strengtheneth me."[321]

[321] Phil. 4:13.

Gerald Vann, O.P.
(1906-1963)

Born in England in 1906, Gerald Vann entered the Dominican Order in 1923 and, after completing his theological studies in Rome, was ordained a priest in 1929. On returning to
England, he studied modern philosophy at Oxford and was
then sent to Blackfriars School in Northhamptonshire to teach
and later to serve as headmaster of the school and superior of
the community there. Tireless in his efforts to bolster the
foundations of peace, he organized the international Union of
Prayer for Peace during his tenure at Blackfriars.

 Fr. Vann devoted his later years to writing, lecturing, and
giving retreats in England and in the United States, including
giving lectures at The Catholic University of America in
Washington, DC.

 He wrote numerous articles and books, including a biogra-
phy of St. Thomas Aquinas, who influenced him greatly. Fr.
Vann's writings combine the philosophy and theology of St.
Thomas with the humanism emphasized in the 1920s and

The Devil

1930s. His works reflect his keen understanding of man's relationship to God, his deep sensitivity to human values, and his compassionate understanding of man's problems and needs. Particularly relevant in today's divided world is his appeal for unity, charity, and brotherhood. His words reveal what it means today to fulfill the two greatest commandments: to love God and to love one's neighbor.

Paul Kevin Meagher, O.P.
(1907-1976)

Paul Kevin Meagher was a priest of the Western Dominican Province in California. Having completed his theological studies at Oxford in 1933, he devoted the next forty years to teaching, most notably at the Dominican House of Studies for the Western Province, where he served as Regent of Studies and Master of Sacred Theology. His research and teaching in the areas of psychology and theology revealed his insights into the mysteries of the human condition, particularly in relation to God.

In 1961, Fr. Meagher began to share these insights through numerous works he co-edited and co-authored, including several works on theology and spirituality, the moral-theology area of the *New Catholic Encyclopedia*, and a translation of the *Summa Theologica* of St. Thomas Aquinas, whose works guided Fr. Meagher throughout his dedicated career as priest, teacher, and writer.

The Devil

Fr. Meagher received the Cardinal Spellman Award from the American Theological Society in 1966 for outstanding work in the area of theological education. He was honored with the degree of Doctor of Divinity at St. Albert's College in California shortly before his death in 1976.

Sophia Institute Press®

Sophia Institute is a nonprofit institution that seeks to restore man's knowledge of eternal truth, including man's knowledge of his own nature, his relation to other persons, and his relation to God.

Sophia Institute Press® serves this end in numerous ways. It publishes translations of foreign works to make them accessible for the first time to English-speaking readers. It brings back into print books that have been long out of print. And it publishes important new books that fulfill the ideals of Sophia Institute. These books afford readers a rich source of the enduring wisdom of mankind.

Sophia Institute Press® makes these high-quality books available to the general public by using advanced technology and by soliciting donations to subsidize its general publishing costs.

Your generosity can help Sophia Institute Press® to provide the public with editions of works containing the enduring wisdom of the ages. Please send your tax-deductible contribution to the address below.

The members of the Editorial Board of Sophia Institute Press® welcome questions, comments, and suggestions from all our readers.

For your free catalog, call:
Toll-free: 1-800-888-9344

or write:
Sophia Institute Press®
Box 5284
Manchester, NH 03108

Internet users may visit our website at
http://www.sophiainstitute.com